What others are saying about the Garden Tutor ...

"It's a great kit for a beginning gardener or an experienced gardener in need of a refresher."

—Ed Hutchison, Syndicated Garden Writer

"If this were a book about golf. I'd say it would take four strokes off your game."

—David Rossi, Binghamton News

"For the beginning gardener, this is a must have."

—Betty Smith, Winchester Sun

"It's a Garden Guru"

—Small Press Magazine

"[T]utor in basics that best educate a gardener. Most of us learn after years of trial and error, so the more information we can get in simple form, the less we'll agonize."

—The News

The Garden Tutor™

Angus Junkin and Chris Knight

Illustrations by James A. Palumbo

Helix Garden Products, Inc.

Garden Tutor™

Angus Junkin and Chris Knight

Illustrations by James A. Palumbo

Cover design by Graphic Workshop, Inc.

Helix Garden Products, Inc.
PO Box 66057, Suite 212
Auburndale, Massachusetts 02166 U.S.A.

ISBN 0-9647331-9-6

Second printing, Revised

Printed and assembled in the United States of America

Table of Contents

Part II: The Process

Appendices

Introduction

Your Key to Successful Gardening!

For many of us gardening is a mystery; we plant things that look good, we are happy if the plants survive, yet we are not surprised when things don't work out the way we wanted. We may read books or speak to others but in the end we still end up relying on intuition to direct us. While this process may lead to successful gardens it usually takes years of experience to develop the confidence and competence to enjoy consistently successful gardens.

The goal of this kit is simple: to give you the skills that a professional gardener would employ without having to invest considerable time or money. This kit will give you the fundamentals of successful gardening, but it will also do much more than that. It will teach you how to evaluate your garden site, how to develop garden styles, how to select plants, and how to care for your garden as well. In short, it will show you the **gardening process:** *how all those little bits of information fit together into a coherent, complete understanding of what it takes to garden with confidence.* That is why the Garden Tutor is the key that unlocks the mysteries of successful gardening.

This kit will help anyone plan and plant a garden site. While there is no substitute for hands-on experience, the systematic approach you learn with this kit will have you experimenting and designing with confidence quickly. Successful gardening requires much more than a good imagination. It requires a working knowledge of the things that constrain a gardener: climate, soil, plants, and maintenance, to name a few.

Introduction

The **Garden Tutor**™ gives you the information and materials you need to understand these constraints, and gives them to you in an easy-to-use kit. The kit includes:

- Our Garden Tutor handbook.
- Enough test strips to perform 10 soil pH tests.
- A compass to help analyze sun exposures.
- A tape measure to use when planting.
- A jar to use when testing soil.
- A soil sample mailing kit for laboratory testing. (We include everything you need to send a sample to a testing laboratory.)

The *handbook* and *components* work together as a unit to help you unlock the mysteries of your garden site. The handbook itself is divided into two parts. *Part I,* **The Elements,** gives you the Garden Tutor program for site analysis, gardening with style, and selecting plants. It will give you a solid foundation for making wise gardening decisions. *Part II,* **The Process,** contains the information you need to install and maintain your garden with confidence and success.

The Garden Tutor is not a complete guide to gardening. We give you the program you need for successful gardening, but we can't begin to include everything there is to know about gardening. Gardening is a learning process. You'll learn a lot from your own experiences, and you can learn more from other books and your gardening friends. In gardening as with most endeavors, the more you learn the better off you will be. And with gardening, the learning can be pleasantly rewarding.

Part I

The Elements

- *Site*
- *Style*
- *Selection*

Site

What is a site?

Your site is the place where plants go: a garden, flower pot, window box, yard. While most people think of a site as just a plot of dirt, it really is more than that: the site includes all of the ingredients that make it unique, such as its soil and climate. Understanding the conditions that make up your site and knowing how to deal with them is crucial to successful gardening. Helping you understand these things is one goal of this kit.

Throughout this book we will refer to a site as that part of your property that is relevant to the project at hand. Sometimes the site will be your whole property, sometimes it will be a particular portion of your property, and sometimes it will be the area around one plant. Hopefully you'll discover that you use the term in a similar fashion: at times it will be convenient for you to call the whole yard your site, and sometimes you'll refer to a flower bed as your site.

How do I determine the conditions on my site?

Site analysis. You will be the detective, gathering data about your site to find out which garden options should work on your site. Site analysis doesn't take much work, yet it is the most important thing you can do to prepare for a garden.

This chapter will take you step-by-step through your site analysis. We discuss the major site-related constraints, and we try to give you helpful information without any fluff. Keep in mind as you read that site analysis isn't perfect: the basic idea we present here is the more you know about your site, the better informed you as a gardener will be. And an informed gardener makes better decisions.

Climate

A climate is an average range of weather conditions in a particular place. This place can be as broad as the entire planet or as small as your backyard. For our purposes climates break down into three levels: *regional*, *area*, and *microclimates*. Regional climates are the broadest you'll need to be concerned with e.g. northeastern United States. Area climates are more specific, usually the area covered by your local news station. Microclimates are site specific— your garden site has its own microclimate, even if the site is just one plant.

As you may see, there is considerable overlap between these levels: the factors that affect your regional climate are similar to those that affect your area climate, just on different scales. The average snowfall in your state probably won't be the same as the snowfall in your backyard.

Regional climate

The regional climate, or at least the regional temperature range, can be determined by referring to the USDA Plant Hardiness Zone Map on page 96. Zones are based on average monthly minimum temperatures, so just know what zone your site is in

Regional Climate

and choose plants that grow in your zone, especially if you order plants by mail. If you purchase plants from local nurseries, chances are good they will grow in your zone, although there are exceptions.

Area Climate

Your area climate is the general area surrounding your site. It includes your town, city, or county. Nearby hills and valleys, large bodies of water, and large metropolitan areas can affect all manner of weather factors. It is then a more accurate measure of what will constrain your gardening decisions than the regional climate because it encompasses a much smaller area.

Area Climate

To determine your area climate, watch local weather reports for trends and pay attention to general descriptions that people use when discussing your area. Descriptions like "the soil in our area is very acidic" or "our weather is affected locally by the wind patterns off Lake Erie" can clue you in to the prevailing conditions in your area. You can also ask your local nursery staff or talk to your gardening friends.

Microclimate

Your microclimate includes all of the conditions specific to your site, and it is your most important gardening constraint. There are many microclimatic variables, and in the rest of this chapter we try to discuss the ones directly relevant to site analysis. *This section contains a lot of important informa-*

Microclimates

tion, most of it basic to successful gardening; any factor discussed in this section can affect your microclimate, and hence your garden.

Soil

Soil is the medium that plants grow in, and it consists of air, moisture, minerals, and organic matter. It also includes the microorganisms that break down organic matter to further enrich the soil. There are many varieties of soil but they are all derived from some combination of sand, silt, and clay; the relative percentages of these minerals determine the soil texture. The soil diagram will show some standard combinations.

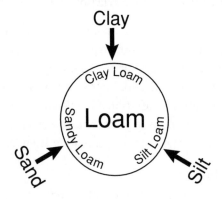

While we classify soil according to its mineral content, plants need more than sand, silt, and clay to thrive. They need air, water, and nutrients. A good soil will have and hold all of these things, based on its **texture** and **structure**.

Soil Texture

Texture refers to the size and distribution of the soil particles, and is most influenced by the mineral content. The texture can tell you a lot about a soil: fine textures, common with clay soils, get compacted easily, and compacted soils don't let much air and water in. Coarse textures, common with sandy soils, let plenty of air and water in but don't hold them well.

Soil Structure

Structure refers to the way soil particles are put together. For practical reasons, think of structure as the shape of the soil particles. The soil minerals bind with the organic matter to form aggregates of various shapes. Some shapes are ideal for holding air and moisture in the soil. Other shapes don't allow enough moisture and air, some allow too much, and some simply don't hold them there long enough to help the plant roots.

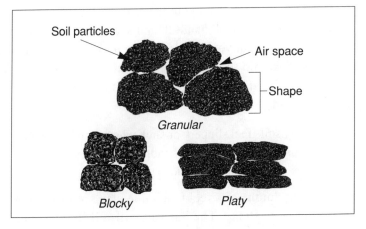

Soil structure

The ideal garden soil is the one that best suits the needs of your plants. Although some plants prefer more extreme soil conditions, the best soil for most plants will be one that has a loamy texture, good granular structure, and plenty of organic matter.

Successful gardens depend on good soil, so the next step is to perform a few easy tests on your soil to determine what type of soil you have. While not everyone will have the "ideal" garden soil you can modify your soil by adding amendments, which are simply things you add to your soil which improve its physical characteristics.

Texture Test (hand method):

Note:

This test will give you a rough approximation of your soil texture. Some soil textures are hard to discriminate based on feel, however.

This test will let you get your hands dirty. Moisten some garden soil, grab a small handful, and squeeze it like a sponge. Knead the soil in your hands and try to roll it between your hands. Then rub some wet soil between your thumb and fingers to judge its grit. Most soils will fit one of the following descriptions:

- **Clay** soils feel slippery or slick when rubbed between your fingers. The sticky handful will not crumble, and it can be rolled into various shapes easily.

- **Clay loam** soils feel much like clay soils only not quite as sticky. The handful will roll into various shapes easily, but will fall apart more readily than straight clay soil.

- **Silty** soils have the texture of the muck found on the bottom of ponds and rivers—at first it feels pretty smooth, but when rubbed between your fingers it has a fine gritty feel. The handful will stay together when squeezed, but crumbles without delicate handling.

- **Sandy loam** soils feel gritty, but the handful can be be worked into a clump that will stay together if handled very delicately.

16

- **Sandy** soils feel very gritty, and you can see the individual sand particles. The handful crumbles quickly.

Since most soils are a mix of these three minerals, the texture test may not be conclusive. The simple jar test can reinforce your texture test results.

Note:

This test should be used in conjunction with the texture test. Neither test is conclusive, but the two together can be helpful.

Jar Test:

(1) Using a garden trowel or spade, dig a small hole (about 6 inches deep) in your site. Slice a sample from the edge of the hole as if you were cutting a thin slice of cake: cut a sliver from top to bottom, using your hand to hold the slice in your trowel or spade. Remove any stones, grass, etc., and put this slice in the enclosed jar. Fill the jar to the soil fill line.

Slicing a soil sample

(2) Add a teaspoon of low-sudsing detergent to the jar, and fill the jar with water. Cap the jar and shake the mixture *vigorously* for 30 seconds. Set the jar down on a level surface.

(3) Leave the jar to settle for a day or two undisturbed.

(4) Unless your soil is straight sand, silt, or clay, you should notice at least two distinguishable layers of soil after the mixture has settled. There may be a third pronounced layer, although usually the middle layer blends into the top and bottom layers.

- The bottom layer will usually be sand. It will be lighter colored than the other layers, and the individual particles should be visible.

- The middle layer will be silt. It tends to blend smoothly into the top and bottom layers, but should be dark-colored with extremely fine particles.

- The top layer should be clay. It will appear as a smooth band, with few (if any) visible particles.

If you have trouble discerning the various layers, you may find it helps to view the jar in good light from a distance of 3 to 5 feet.

(5) Measure the thickness of each layer and the entire sample. Divide the thickness of each layer by the thickness of the entire sample. Multiply each result by 100, and you will have the rough percentages of sand, silt, and clay that comprise your soil. Match your results to the chart to find out your soil texture type.

For example: if your sand layer is 1 inch thick and the entire sample is 3 inches thick, divide 1 by 3 to get .33, then multiply this by 100 to get 33%.

Soil Texture Classifications*

Soil Texture	% Sand	% Silt	% Clay
Clay	0-45	0-40	40-100
Sand	85-100	0-15	0-10
Silt	0-20	80-100	0-12
Loam	23-52	27-50	7-27
Loamy Sand	70-85	0-30	0-15
Sandy Loam	43-85	0-50	0-20
Sandy Clay Loam	45-80	0-27	20-35
Silt Loam	0-50	50-100	0-27
Silty Clay Loam	0-20	40-71	27-40
Clay Loam	20-45	17-52	27-40
Sandy Clay	45-65	0-20	35-55
Silty Clay	70-88	0-30	10-14

*Based on USDA soil classifications. Some percentages have been approximated.

Note:

One common misconception is that if a soil is compacted it must be clay. This is not always the case. Any soil can be compacted, clay simply compacts much easier than other soil types.

If your soil composition is out of proportion for loam, you can compensate for this by adding various soil amendments to help improve soil structure. There are two things to remember, though: **(1)** you will need to add a lot of whatever you add to make a noticeable change in soil composition, and **(2)** improving your soil structure takes time. The process is very gradual, although the speed at which soil structure changes can be affected by the type of amendment(s) you use.

Note:

While it is possible to change soil texture by adding sand, vermiculite, or clay, the material and energy involved is considerable. Further, if you do not add enough of these substances to your soil there will be no positive effect on soil texture. In fact, adding too little sand to clay soil can actually make matters worse.

The amendment of choice is good compost, aged manure, or an improved top soil. Because these are rich in organic content and very broken down already, they will bind with your existing soil faster than other amendments and they will sustain your plants until the soil structure has been changed. You can use raw organic matter like leaves, bark, or peat moss, but it will take longer to affect the soil structure; the raw amendments must finish composting in the soil before they bind. Still, since raw organic matter takes longer to break down its effects often last longer. Whichever type you use, keep in mind that plants will benefit from annual additions of organic matter.

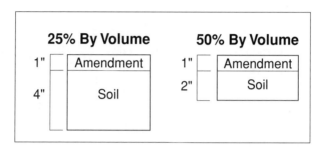

If your jar test reveals that you have a straight clay, silt, or sand soil you can add up to 50% by volume of an amendment to the soil. If your soil falls into one of the other categories (as most soils will) then add up to 25% by volume of an amendment to achieve a good mix. When you are amending a bare site, work the amendments fully into the soil by tilling or otherwise turning the soil (see **Preparation**). If the site already has established plants, put the amendment on top of the soil and gently rake it into the surface.

A precise soil blend is not needed, by the way. Just try to get it close. As we'll remind you often in this book, most plants are remarkably flexible with respect to soil texture and other variables. There are soils they definitely thrive in, but they'll at least grow in most soils.

Soil Horizons

For gardening purposes we are usually concerned with the top 6-10 inches of soil because most plants (from a Rose to a Redwood) will have their feeding roots close to the surface where most of the moisture and nutrients are. Below the 6-10 inch layer of fertile soil are other layers called horizons. Soil horizons are bands of differing soils that change with depth. These changes can be in color (darker

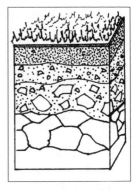

Soil horizons

shades indicate more organic material), hardness, and type. Soil horizons tend to be more fertile at the surface and less fertile the deeper they go.

Generally, soil horizons are a concern only if you have a drainage problem or very limited topsoil. This is common around newly-constructed homes where soil has been compacted by construction equipment and a thin layer of loam was spread over it after construction. If your soil stays wet or you have standing puddles for a few days after a good rainfall, you can either modify your horizon to improve drainage (see **Appendix 2**) or find plants that can deal with this condition.

Disturbed soils occur when infertile soil horizons are mixed in with more fertile topsoil. Backhoes and bulldozers are prime soil disturbers. If you have disturbed soil you may need to adjust and amend it to sustain healthy plants.

pH

pH stands for potential hydrogen, and it can tell you a lot about your soil. For your purposes think of it as potential nutrients—pH determines which nutrients are available to plants. In fact, pH affects the microorganism activity in your soil. Soil pH determines its acidity (sourness) or alkalinity (sweetness). The lower the pH, the more acidic your soil is; the higher the pH the more alkaline it is. The neutral range for the pH scale is around 6.5, and most plants prefer a soil pH between 6 and 7. Some plants prefer more acidic or alkaline soils, but for general gardening all that matters is that your soil not be *too* acidic or alkaline unless the plants you select can tolerate these conditions. Plants are very flexible with respect to pH, so long as your site isn't near the extremes of acidity or alkalinity for the particular plants.

If your soil pH is too extreme for your plants, it creates an unhealthy environment by limiting the nourishment that is available to the plants *and* by weakening their natural defenses against pestilence and disease.

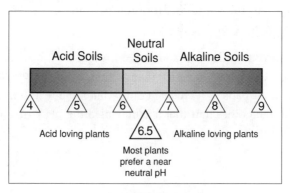

pH Scale for gardeners

The pH Test:

Note:

This test should be performed separately from the jar test. The detergent used in the jar test can affect your pH reading.

The pH test is a simple indicator test requiring some soil, water, the plastic jar, and a pH strip. The pH strips have two pads on them, each pad covering a specific pH range. The Green (top) pad covers a range of 3.5-5.5 and the Orange (bottom) pad covers a range of 5-9.

(1) Collect soil samples the same way you did for the jar test. Clean the jar, then add soil to the soil fill line.

(2) Fill the rest of the jar with water, cap the jar, and shake it vigorously for about 30 seconds.

(3) Wait 10 seconds, and then dip one pH strip into the solution. Hold the strip in the solution for 3 seconds.

(4) Remove the pH strip and shake it vigorously to remove any dirt. One or both of the color pads will change color. Match the resulting color(s) with the color chart that accompanied the pH strips to determine your soil pH.

pH strip

For more accurate results, you can use distilled water for the test. We have included enough indicator for 10 tests, so you may want to test various parts of your site individually to see if there are variations within your garden. Annual tests are useful, too.

Before you can adjust your soil pH you should know your soil type, so perform the jar test first. Your soil type can affect the quantity of pH amendment (lime or sulfur) you use. You should also be aware that it takes a lot of amendments to change pH.

Lowering pH If you need a more acidic soil you can use sulfur or naturally acidic organic materials (peat moss, leaves and needles from acidic plants). If you use organic material the pH change will be very gradual; if you are in a hurry you may opt for sulfur. It is best not to use commercial plant acidifiers containing aluminum sulfates or fertilizers containing ammonia to alter soil pH; they are best used only to maintain plants already growing in acidic soil, and misuse can ruin your soil.

Raising pH The best way to raise soil pH is to add lime. Lime is readily available and easy to apply. You may have a few types of lime to choose from depending what retailers in your area carry. Pulverized or pelletized limestone is usually a good choice (pelletized lime can be used in a broadcast spreader). Dolomitic limestone is limestone which contains magnesium and a few other trace nutrients. You can use ground limestone, just be aware that it is a powder, and powders are harder to apply with a broadcast spreader. Hydrated limes are also available; they work quickly but can burn plants and flesh if used incorrectly. In any case, be sure to follow the application

Applying lime with a broadcast spreader

rates and package instructions *strictly*. If you add too much at one time you can harm your plants and your soil.

The following charts will give you approximate application rates. If the chart disagrees with the label on the product you buy, always go with the manufacturer guidelines. Adjusting soil pH with lime and sulfur is not permanent so you'll need to recheck soil pH every year or two and make adjustments as necessary. The degree and duration of the change depends on how finely ground the amendments are (lime and sulfur). The more finely ground (e.g. pulverized) the faster they alter pH but shorter their effects last (generally 1-2 years depending on your climate). Note that pelletized lime is finely ground but aggregated with a binding agent to form easy to spread pellets. It is best to apply lime and sulfur in the fall or early spring, so they can start working on your soil before you plant.

A few general facts about soil pH:

• Clay soils tend to be acidic

• Sandy soils tend to be alkaline

• Keeping pH at the proper level for the plants in your garden will help reduce garden pests and diseases.

• Lime helps improve the structure of the soil

Lime Chart: Pulverized Lime*

To raise to pH to 6.5   **Soil Texture**

Current Soil pH	Sand	Loam	Clay
6.0	2.0 lbs	3.5 lbs	5.0 lbs
5.5	4.5 lbs	7.5 lbs	10 lbs
5.0	6.5 lbs	11 lbs	15 lbs
4.5	8.0 lbs	15 lbs	20 lbs
4.0	10 lbs	17.5 lbs	23 lbs

* Application rates based on pounds per 100 square feet.

Sulfur Chart: Granular Sulfur*

To lower pH to 6.5   **Soil Texture**

Current Soil pH	Sand	Loam	Clay
8.5	3.5 lbs	4.0 lbs	4.5 lbs
8.0	2.5 lbs	3.0 lbs	3.5 lbs
7.5	1.5 lbs	2.0 lbs	2.5 lbs
7.0	1.0 lbs	1.5 lbs	2.0 lbs

* Application rates based on pounds per 100 square feet.

Nutrients

Nutrients are essential for plant growth. Of the sixteen nutrients needed for healthy plant growth, three merit special attention. A few others called intermediate nutrients (calcium, magnesium, and sulfur) are needed only if your soil is known to lack them; they are usually supplied when you adjust your soil pH. The rest are trace nutrients (micronutrients) that are present in most soils.

The common nutrients Nitrogen (**N**), Phosphorus (**P**), and Potassium (**K**) are the prevailing ingredients in most fertilizers, and can be purchased in dry or liquid form. Note that dry fertilizers require fewer applications and last longer than liquid fertilizers, although liquid fertilizers produce faster results. There are many fertilizers on the market, and it is very important to understand the labeling. There should be three large numbers on the label (example: 5-10-5) corresponding to the percentages of nitrogen, phosphorous, and potassium.

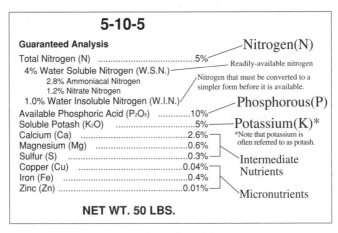

Sample fertilizer label.

In most cases, you will want what is called a balanced fertilizer, which has roughly equal proportions of N, P, and K. An exception to this general rule: if a laboratory soil analysis shows your soil overwhelmingly deficient in a particular nutrient, you may want to use either a straight fertilizer (with only the lacking nutrient) or a complete fertilizer that is unbalanced in favor of the deficient nutrient. Also, some plants have specific fertilizer requirements. Potatoes, for instance, will produce small tubers if they get too much nitrogen.

A final note on fertilizers: they come in organic and in-organic types. Organic fertilizers usually consist of decom-posed organic matter (compost, manure, fish scrap, seaweed) that finishes breaking down after you apply it, while inorganic *Organic* fertilizers are usually chemically-refined organic matter. *vs* *Inorganic* Organics often have much lower concentrations of N, P, and K than inorganics. Both give plants the nutrients they need but inorganics are more readily available to plants, especially dur-ing climactic extremes when the microorganisms that break down organic fertilizers in your soil are dormant.

Over the long run, you should use either organic fertilizers or a combination of organic and inorganic fertilizers to help maintain proper nutrient balance and continually improve the quality of your soil. Organic fertilizers are much harder to overuse (because they are less concentrated) and they either contain or promote beneficial organisms that help build your soil and fight harmful pests and diseases. Complete reliance on inorganic fertilizer leads to just that: complete reliance. If you don't replenish the soil's organic content, you will have to fertilize often. In general, organics improve your environment by keeping the soil fertile.

Soil Testing

The tests we have discussed are very useful for determining your site conditions. Still, you may want to consider having a laboratory soil analysis performed before you plant and then every few years after that. A laboratory test can give you more detail about the nutritional state of your garden, but more importantly it can alert you to soil contamination. If you plan to grow plants for consumption, or live in an area with old houses that may have leaded paint on them, we strongly recommend a laboratory soil test.

To have your soil tested:

(1) You will need a representative sample of your garden soil. Get samples just as you did for the jar test, but get more of them from different parts of your site. Mix the soil sample thoroughly in a clean bucket and eliminate any foreign debris.

(2) Address the enclosed soil sample envelope.

(3) Fill out the soil sample information on the back of the envelope. This is important, because often the testing agency can make specific evaluations based on the plants you want to grow in your garden.

(4) Pour about 2 cups of your thoroughly-mixed sample in the bag, place the bag in the mailing envelope, enclose payment, and mail it. The soil testing lab will send back a report showing your soil nutrient levels along with any necessary fertilizer application rates.

Sun

Adequate sunlight for plants is essential, if they don't get the sunlight they need they simply will not grow well. There are two things about the sun you need to know for your site analysis: the path and amount.

Path

First, you need to know the sun's path over your property. To do this use the enclosed compass to find East and West. The sun will rise from the East and set to the West. Once you know the sun's

Sun Intensity*	
Full Sun	6 plus hrs
Part Sun	4 to 6 hrs
Part Shade	2 to 4 hrs
Full Shade	0 to 2 hrs

*Figures are for direct sunlight

Amount

general path over your site, look for East-to-West areas that are sunny and shaded at various times of the day. Make a note of the sun exposures. The levels are: full sun, part sun, part shade, and full shade. (see **chart**)

Next, you need to determine how the sun's path changes with the seasons. The sun is highest during the summer solstice, lowest during the winter solstice and between these points during the fall and spring equinoxes.

The degree of change depends on your latitude: the farther north you are, the greater the shift. The closer you are to the equator, the smaller the shift. (If you are very close to the

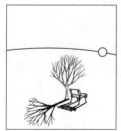

Winter solstice
(Dec. 21)

Equinox
(Mar. 21/Sep. 21)

Summer solstice
(Jun. 21)

equator, you don't need to read this section!)

You should spend some time determining how this southern shift will affect the amount of sun your garden receives at different times of the year. Account for seasonal shadows based on the sun shift, and determine which parts of your site get how much sunlight. Knowing these things will help you select and place plants appropriate for your microclimate.

While it may seem a bit time consuming, try to draw a rough sketch of the summer and winter shady areas based on the path of the sun. You don't need much precision; just try to get close. It can be a heartbreaker to invest a lot of time and money into a garden only to discover that it is full shade for half of the year. Some careful attention to the sun and its relation to your site will help you avoid situations like this, and will help you select plants that can thrive all year.

Now, having said that a lot of precision isn't necessary, it bears saying that the more you know about the sun exposures on your site, the better you can plant with success. In **Appendix 3** we provide detailed information and charts so you can calculate sun exposures precisely, if you are so inclined.

General sunlight hints:
- Southern exposures are best for vegetables and plants that require lots of sun.
- Northern exposures receive the least sun.
- Morning sun is usually less intense than afternoon sun, so eastern exposures receive slightly less sunlight than western exposures.
- Between 10 and 2 P.M. the sun is at peak intensity. Plants that need full sun may thrive if they get direct sunlight during this time.

Specific Conditions

Wind

There are prevailing wind patterns and inconsistent wind patterns. Prevailing wind patterns are relatively constant. An ocean breeze is a good example: over the course of a year this wind pattern may remain roughly the same or change with the seasons, but it is a regular feature of your climate. If you have a particularly strong or severe prevailing wind pattern, account for it when selecting plants and their placement. Delicate plants are badly affected by strong wind, and some plants are sensitive to winter wind burn (especially broadleaf evergreens).

Inconsistent wind patterns occur infrequently, usually during storms. There isn't a lot you can do about the ravages of nature, but if you live in an area prone to violent storms you may want to pay very close attention to the location of your BIG plants, especially the ones that can blow over and damage your life or your property. Shallow rooted trees near a house can be a real hazard if you live in a tornado zone, for instance. Any tree limbs near a window or hanging over your house can be a source of property damage as well.

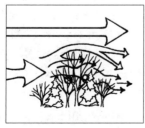
Trees with open canopies reduce wind velocity.

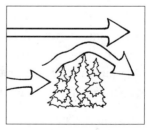
Thick foliage and dense groups of trees divert wind.

Wind can either be reduced or diverted. Reducing wind requires structures that filter the wind: trees, shrubs, and structures such as lattice, when placed properly, do this well. Thick groups of trees or shrubs with dense foliage will divert the wind rather than reduce its velocity. So will structures like buildings, fences, and walls (see **next section**).

Structure

Trees, shrubs, slopes, outcroppings, hollows, buildings, fences, eaves, and walls make up the structure on your site. Structure can affect wind, sun, soil, and temperature conditions, and *all* these can affect plant selection and placement. Structure can be especially relevant when it is large: houses and large trees can have profound effects on sun and wind patterns, and in some climates can be responsible for large amounts of snow or rain shedding off the edges. As well, some trees and shrubs have very invasive root systems that can affect the soil conditions on your site by competing with new plants for moisture and nutrients. Take these structures into account when selecting and placing plants.

When designing your garden site, bear in mind that what you plant may itself become a microclimate-affecting structure. Small trees get bigger over time, and what was once a full sun part of your site may be full shade in ten years. Also, your choice of plants can affect your soil: for example, years of falling pine needles can make your soil acidic which in turn can affect any plants in the vicinity.

Determining what influence structure will have on wind patterns is not easy. If applicable, notice how snow or leaf drifts form around your property. Areas where bare ground is exposed when the rest of your site has snow or leaf coverage give hints about your wind patterns. If you plan to add structures to your site, try to anticipate how they will affect your wind patterns and place plants where they won't be damaged. Otherwise, just remember to be concerned about safety if you live in a harsh, stormy climate—trees too close to houses and power lines can be hazardous under some conditions.

You can remove tree branches or whole trees if you want to get more sunlight into an area (see **Pruning**). When removing trees put some thought into it and don't make hasty decisions—you can't get that graceful Oak back after you've chopped it down.

Caution

Unless you are a skilled arborist, you should consult with a tree service before removing large trees or tree limbs.

Variables

Variables are factors that may or may not affect your site. *This list is by no means comprehensive*, but we tried to get the most important ones:

Utilities

You should know whether any underground cables and pipelines run through your site before you do any digging. You can find out by calling the various utility companies involved, but the best thing to do is contact your local utility-locating service.

Check your phone directory or call your state public utilities commission. This service should be provided free.

Bear in mind that if you damage a utility cable or pipeline without calling such a service you may be liable for any resulting damage.

Also, if you have an overhead power line you'll want to plan accordingly, i.e., don't plant a tree that will interfere with a power line.

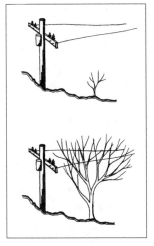

Don't plant trees under power lines.

Shallow Soil

You should test your soil depth in the areas you will be planting. If you have only a few inches of soil before you run into bedrock, you will have to either (1) install plants that can tolerate this condition, or (2) consider planting in raised beds. Either way, your nursery staff can recommend plants for this condition. Be aware also that many shallow soil sites have drainage or runoff problems which you may have to solve as well.

Wet Sites

Too much ground moisture can suffocate many plants. If your site is very close to the water table you may have to select plants that can tolerate a lot of moisture. Sites near ponds, streams, and swamps can be very moist throughout the year; sometimes the water table is high even though there is no surface water nearby, and that keeps the soil very moist.

Some areas are prone to seasonal moisture due to heavy rains and flooding. If you are blessed with such a site, try to determine the average affected area and select plants that can tolerate your conditions. See **Appendix 2** for details about drainage solutions.

Your nursery can suggest plants that are suited to overly moist conditions.

Salt

If you live near a seashore or near roads that are salted during the winter, your plants can suffer salt damage. Salt spray can burn or kill plants (especially evergreens) so be aware of the salt exposure on your site and plant accordingly, or use an anti-desiccant on evergreens (see **Winterizing**). Winter salt spray tends to affect areas close to the roadside; seashore salt spray tends to affect all of your soil. See **Appendix 1** for details about special conditions.

Legal Considerations

Before undertaking any major landscaping on your site, check for local codes that may restrict fences, walls, or plant locations. Know exactly where your property boundary is, and by all means discuss your plans with your neighbors. All of these things can help prevent a BIG headache after you finish your project.

Animals

Deer, rabbits, woodchucks, moles, and pets can be nice to have around, but they probably want to nibble on your beautiful plants, excrete in your lawn, or dig up your bulbs. Think about how you will handle these problems when you design your garden, not afterwards. Fences, repellents, repellent plants, and your ingenuity can control unwanted visitors.

You may find it nice to have a garden that attracts the local wildlife. Just remember: once you invite the animals in, they will not want to leave just because you are tired of them eating your bulbs. If you want animals and try to attract them, be sure you won't change your mind later. After the local wildlife has tasted your garden, it's much harder to discourage them from coming back.

Also, be cautious with all wild animals. They can bite, and they can be rabid.

Putting it all together

Site analysis determines the **growing conditions** on your site. With a little detective work you can discover what your site needs to sustain a healthy garden. Here is a recap of the key steps in a site analysis.

Regional Climate

❑ Determine your **regional climate** by referring to the USDA hardiness zone map on page 96. This will help you select plants that grow in your region.

Area Climate

❑ Determine your **area climate** by finding out about prevailing conditions in your area.

Microclimate

Soil:

❑ Perform soil texture tests using the instructions in this chapter. If your soil doesn't have a good texture and structure, you can amend your soil by adding organic matter.

❑ Check soil depth, compaction, and condition of soil horizons by digging a 1-2' hole. If necessary, make drainage corrections or add organic material.

❑ Perform soil pH test as described in the chapter. This is vital, because soil pH can tell you a lot about the nutritional state of your soil. If necessary, adjust soil pH by adding lime (to raise pH) or sulfur (to lower pH).

❏ Have soil tested for nutritional needs and contaminants. Add nutrients using either organic or inorganic fertilizer, depending on your site needs.

Sun:

❏ Determine the east-west sun path across your site, using your compass. This will help you find areas that will be shaded or exposed to the sun throughout the course of the day. Don't rely on intuition here: use the compass, you will be surprised at the results.

❏ Figure the amount of sun exposure so you can select plants that will thrive under those sunlight conditions. You can do this by observation, or you can refer to **Appendix 3** if you want pinpoint accuracy.

Specific Conditions:

❏ Pay close attention to your **wind** patterns. Depending on your area and microclimate, winds can have a dramatic effect on delicate plants. For instance, if your site is prone to strong, cold winds in the wintertime, you'll want to select hardy plants that can cope with this condition.

❏ **Structures**, both natural *and* man-made, can profoundly modify your site. Consider the effect they have on wind patterns, soil depth, snow/rain shedding, and shading.

Style

What is Style?

Style can be many things to many people. For you it will be
the unique way you arrange the materials that will make up
your garden. Usually, creating garden designs with style is a
compromise between your **wants** and your **constraints**. Wants
will vary from person to person. A family with six energetic
children might desire hardiness over aesthetics. A retired
couple may want a more aesthetic garden. A homeowner in a
new suburban neighborhood may want just *anything* to cover
the dirt left by the developer. So wants can range from merely
functional to wildly biodiverse landscapes.

Theme

It is common for gardens to have a theme around which the
style is developed. Themes can be simple, as those based on a
particular plant type or color. They can be complex, based on
a particular period or trend. Whatever the theme may be, it
can help unify your garden design by tying the various parts
together. As well, it can help you decide on a style.

Whichever style you opt for, here are some stylistic tenets that
gardeners should be aware of. Although these fundamentals
may seem obvious to some, others may find this information
welcome:

There is no ultimate garden design

The first rule of garden design is that there is no ultimate garden design. Your garden design should fit your site and your
wants. There may be several wonderful designs that accom-
plish this. Your goal should be a garden that does what you
want it to do and looks the way you want it to look.

Our goal is to help you achieve that goal. While there isn't an ultimate garden design, there are successful and unsuccessful gardens!

Garden design takes time and vision

The notion of deferring your gratification is no better demonstrated than by gardening. Five years will pass quickly in retrospect, and remembering this when you plant can enhance your garden. Gardens grow and evolve, and you want to anticipate the *mature* growth of your plants. Resisting the temptation to fill in between plants that have been properly spaced when young will pay big dividends in aesthetic and personal satisfaction when they mature.

Focus on the design, not the plants

More often than not, plant arrangement is more important than the plants: if you just plant a bunch of your favorite plants, you will have a garden which is limited to a jumble of your favorite plants. If you design your garden and choose plants that are appropriate to your constraints and theme, you can have a healthy, interesting, and beautiful garden.

Nothing is etched in stone

From time to time you may see a mistake in the design of your garden or selection of your plants. Sometimes a plant won't thrive, or it doesn't fit in the way you hoped. Before losing any sleep you should look at your discovery as a positive experience. Simply put, not all gardening mistakes are bad and usually all of them are learning opportunities. Often you can correct things easily, and over time your tastes may change in favor of the 'mistake'. If a particular plant type keeps dying, try to find out why. Or try a different plant. If something looks out of place, move it. Don't be afraid to change and experiment. That is often the real joy of gardening, and you can get a lot of gardening wisdom by dealing with adversity.

Look at other gardens

If you see a garden design that someone else has created and you like it there is nothing wrong with borrowing ideas from it. Then you can enhance or personalize it as your site requires. You may like the selection of plant materials or just the curves that were used in another design. You can let other gardens inspire your creativity—you have to start somewhere.

Learn about plants

The more plants you are familiar with the better you will be able to choose plants that fit your design requirements. Also, the more plants you know the more creative you can be. Books, magazines, newspaper articles, and friendly suggestions can help considerably. In gardening as with most things, knowledge is power. Anything that can supplement your experience should be welcomed.

Scale

A sense of scale can help when designing a garden. Keep the *relative sizes* and *distances* of the plants in mind, because the way plants fit into their surroundings can have a dramatic effect on the viewer. The goal should be to balance both the scale of the objects in your landscape to each other and to the viewer. There are no hard and fast rules here—you have to be the judge. Still, keep some notion of scale in your designing arsenal; subtle attention to it can pay big rewards later, when the garden matures.

Scale depends heavily on the *viewing perspective*, so try to think like a photographer: Determine a fixed viewing area (a porch, picture window, curbside) and view your garden site through a picture frame or a camera lens. Look for things that seem out of proportion e.g. large trees near a small house, small flowers hidden in a large bed, a huge tree too close to your viewing window, where all but the trunk is obscured. All of these things and more can disturb the 'picture'.

A photographer will arrange things to capture a balanced, stimulating image. As a garden designer, you can do the same thing: you can choose plants and locations that bring the picture into proportion. When you plant beds, arrange taller plants in back, shorter ones in front, and step up the height gradually. If there is a noticeable gap in the viewing window that demands attention, fill it with something. If you have a large plant or structure that dominates your site, try to draw attention away from it with clever visual distractions.

Of course, in most cases you will have constraints. You probably can't move your house, and you may not want to remove that big tree growing next to the garage. You may get a good scale from one perspective but not from another. Sometimes your site leaves you with little room to work with. Our suggestion is to acknowledge what you can't change, blend in some imagination, and work with the stuff you can change. Do your best and you won't go wrong; any attention to proper scale is better than none at all.

Symmetry

In general, *symmetry* involves mirror-imaging: items are symmetrical if their parts are uniformly balanced and spaced on each side of a dividing line. Items which are not symmetric are *asymmetric*. In gardening, symmetry implies formality, and asymmetry implies informality.

Formal and Informal

Strict formality requires control, order, and symmetry: straight lines, perfect balance, and repetition of geometric patterns. Strictly speaking, informality entails an asymmetric variety of freeform shapes in a random order. Most gardeners try to balance the extremes by blending some formal characteristics with a few informal ones. Thus you may have sharp lines and nearly symmetrical arrangements with some variety and contrast thrown in to make the garden comfortable and pleasing.

45

One general rule to be aware of: formal styles are well-suited close to a house, and informal styles work well farther from the house. The formality nearby helps relate the rigid lines of the house to the surrounding landscape.

Simplicity

Simplicity when designing can be good. While you don't want to overdo it, deliberate spacing, uncluttered beds, repetition of plants, and simple lines can enhance your garden and make it easy for the viewer to appreciate it. It also helps the viewer discern subtle changes in style as they are lead through the garden.

We mention this because many people tend to cram lots of everything into their garden sites, and after the first year they find that the garden is too crowded to work in, the plants don't mature as fast because they are cramped, and when the blooms are finished the garden looks like a big, cluttered mess.

Variety

A garden with a broad assortment of plants and arrangements can be a genuine delight. A variety of different plants can open new doors to contrast and beauty. After you have decided on a theme and style for your garden, try to select a variety of plant shapes and sizes that fit your theme and your site constraints. You don't want to overdo it, though. Keep your design simple, but remember that variety can be the spice of your garden.

On the same note, try to find creative garden uses for interesting terrain features. That rock outcrop may look like an

eyesore, but with some imagination you can turn it into a pleasing garden. Sometimes it is better to enhance the unusual features of a landscape rather than remove them and start from scratch. Remember, though, that if you want to use that terrain feature to your advantage then don't design something which covers it up or detracts from it.

Rooms

If you have a large site, you may want to break it up into rooms or compartments. The rooms in your house may have different styles and tones, and your garden can be like that as well. You may have a formal room, an informal room, a tea room, a solitude room. Fences and other structure can help enclose various rooms, but you can make rooms simply by having different themes in different parts of your site.

Deception

When designing gardens, you may want to create impressions that deceive: the small wooded patch in your backyard can give the appearance of a large wooded patch; a path that looks like a peaceful stroll to Eden may just lead to your pool filtration system. Hide air conditioning systems, electrical conduit boxes, and other eyesores with a few well-placed plants. By being creative, you can mask many of your site constraints and create a nice retreat.

Choose plants for all seasons

Many plants look good throughout the year. A deciduous shrub may have nice foliage and blooms during the growing season while in the winter it may have berries that attract birds. Some perennials look good even when dormant. Dead stalks and flowers can add a nice touch to the landscape during the bleak winter months.

Arrangement

Beds and Borders

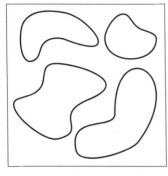
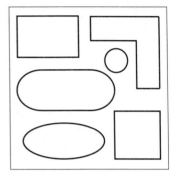

Freeform beds   *Geometric beds*

Beds and borders frame your garden by defining its size and shape. When creating natural gardens (i.e. woodland gardens or desert gardens) you may not want to use them; just let the plants fit the land forms. Beds and borders are more effective around a house or other large structure since they help relate your landscape to it. There are two types of beds, freeform and geometric. As you might expect, the former is more informal and the latter is formal. Below are some tips for both.

Lines

Keep lines simple and avoid too many changes in direction. Also, keep lines sharp—good edging creates a strong visual impression.

Curves

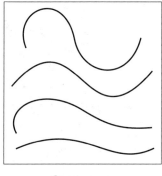 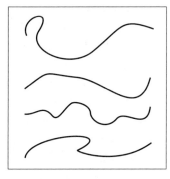

Good curves   Bad curves

You may want to use curves when creating garden beds or borders. Curves can have a powerful effect when used properly because they help your site stand out. Here are some points to remember:

(1) Let curves fit the terrain—the terrain may lend itself toward a particular curve; try to identify that curve and exploit it.

(2) Keep curves simple—too many curves (especially wavy curves) can create a mess that is hard on the viewer.

(3) Keep curves subtle and smooth—abrupt curves are less effective visually than smooth curves.

(4) Use a hose to determine which curves you like best.

Plants

Specimen

When you plant a single plant which is large enough to stand alone and not get lost in the background you are specimen planting. You can specimen plant to highlight plants, either by themselves or in a mixed planting (such as in a perennial garden). Plants chosen for specimen planting usually have characteristics that help them stand out nicely.

Specimen

Grouping

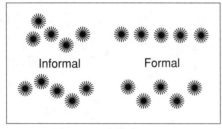

Informal   Formal

Plant arrangements

Grouping

For grouping, plant with either a uniform or staggered layout (diagram). Grouping highlights plants that when planted alone are not big enough to stand out. Unlike massing, however, a group highlights the individual plants as well. Arrange it so there is a delicate balance between the plant shape and the shape of the overall group.

Massing

Massing allows you to highlight a particular area of your property. It lends itself toward simplicity and is very effective when used with plants that by themselves or in small groups would become lost in the background. Massing helps bring large sites into scale as well, since a massed group seen from a distance can help fill a void on your garden 'canvas'. (see **Scale**)

Massing

When massing the individual plant yields to the overall shape of the mass. Thus it is the shape of the whole planting that you emphasize.

Tip:

Triangle plantings can unify a garden very effectively. Use three plants that will stand out a bit from the rest of the planting and arrange them in a triangle. Any triangle will do; the closer the arrangement is to an isosceles triangle, the more formal the arrangement will be.

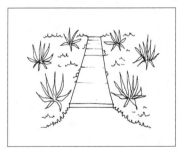

Formal

Informal

51

Texture

Texture refers to the visual 'feel' of a plant. You can take advantage of differently-textured plants to create contrasts, define a space, or set a theme for your garden.

Small-leafed or needled plants are considered fine textured; they have a soft appearance and appear blurry

Use textures to create a sense of space.

when viewed from afar. The fine texture helps create a sense of space.

Large-leafed plants have a coarse texture. These usually stand out when viewed from afar, and they tend to make spaces look smaller.

Color

Color can be used for a few important purposes. It creates a sense of space, it can help you create themes, and in general it makes a garden psychologically uplifting. It's good to use colors as a guideline in design but don't worry about it too much—it's very hard to wreck a garden with improper color use. In fact, it's hard to know just what would constitute improper color use!

NEUTRAL COLORS

Transitional colors which enhance your dominant colors: White helps tie lighter shades together, although it can also create strong contrasts between darker colors. White effectively brightens some shady areas, also.

Gray and silver foliage makes an excellent transition between different shades of green foliage.

WARM COLORS

Approaching colors. They jump out and welcome you: reds, oranges, and yellows.

COOL COLORS

Receding colors. They pull away and leave you with a soft sense of space: blues, purples, and greens.

COLOR SCHEMES

Monochromatic: Using a single color and its various shades.

Polychromatic: Using different colors for contrast and balance.

Color Complements: Blending only warm or cool colors and their various shades together.

Color Contrasts: Mixing cool colors with warm colors. Experiment with various contrasts and you will be pleasantly surprised with the result.

Color isn't just about flowers

Creating Contrasts

Most of the time you'll be looking at the foliage and bark of a non-blooming plant, so be sure to consider the whole plant and not just the blooms. Incidentally, the foliage and bark color along with the shape and texture of the plant can be put to very effective use when designing. Subtle contrasts in all of these factors can have a powerful impact on your garden.

Putting it all together

In this chapter we discussed the elements of creating a garden design with style. It is important to remember there is no one perfect design. As you experiment with different designs and plants you will see that many different approaches work well for your site. The raw materials of garden design that we discuss in this chapter will help you experiment with confidence:

❑ Determine your **wants** and **constraints** (site analysis).

❑ Choose a **theme** garden of shapes, textures, etc. Decide how formal/informal you want your garden to be, and plan your design accordingly. Use beds, borders, lines and plants creatively to establish your theme.

❑ Keep your garden in focus with proper **scale**. When designing, anticipate the *mature growth* of your plants and bring the various parts of your garden into focus for the main viewing areas.

❑ **Simplicity** and **repetition** are *very* important. Too much complexity detracts from the harmony of your garden.

❑ **Variety** is the spice of your garden. It creates contrasts of color, texture, and height that can really enhance your garden. Note that variety isn't the same as complexity; you can use simplicity and variety together with nice results.

❑ Be creative with your plant **arrangements**. Create color and texture contrasts based on flowers, foliage, and shape.

Selection

You will probably get plants and seeds from retail garden centers (nurseries) or from mail order retailers. Large nurseries usually have a wide range of plants; smaller garden centers usually have a smaller stock of plants to choose from, but you can often find a more relaxed and helpful sales staff. Mail order suppliers may carry hard to find or unique plants, and anything else you want as well.

Nursery stock should be labeled. A good label will tell you the basics: how and when to plant, proper spacing, and the plant's hardiness zone. It should also list any special features (color, texture, size, etc.) that plant has.

Geranium sanguineum var. lancastriense
Perennial
Hardy Geranium

Light Pink flowers with scarlet veins. Blooms May to September. Good border or rock garden plant.

How to Grow:
Plant in full to part sun. Does well in most garden soils. Space 12-15". Grows 6-10".

Zones 4-10

A typical nursery label.

The following is a brief description of the major plant categories that you will come across at the nursery. At the most general level plants break down into two groups: **woody** and **non-woody** plants. The subdivisions are listed below.

Note that some plants are usually considered separately from the basic categories, either because they are very popular or because they have some special characteristic that they have become known by. Some of these plants are roses, herbs, vegetables, edible berries, groundcovers, shade plants, and vines.

Plant Types

Woody

Deciduous shrubs

Woody plants that lose their leaves at the end of the growing season are deciduous. Some offer dazzling floral displays before most other plants emerge in the Spring. Many shrubs bloom at other times of the growing season, so you can choose them based on their bloom period to fill gaps when many other plants are past their blooms. Some shrubs have interesting foliage and/or bark, so you can choose them for texture contrasts as well.

Semi-evergreen

These are plants that may or may not lose their leaves, depending on your climate. In many instances there are shrubs that are usually deciduous but in southern climates are truly evergreen.

Evergreen shrubs

Shrubs that do not lose their leaves count as evergreens. These include broad-leafed, narrow-leafed, and needled evergreens. They are good to have in wintry climates.

Deciduous trees

Same as deciduous shrubs, except trees are larger.

Evergreen Trees

Same as evergreen shrubs, except trees are larger.

Non-Woody

Annuals

Annuals live for only one growing season. They bloom profusely throughout the growing season, and usually last until the first major frost in your area. You will have to replace them annually, hence the name. They are primarily chosen for their flowers but in some cases for their foliage color and texture, because they provide continuous color throughout their growing season.

They are most effective when massed or grouped.

Biennials

These are good bloomers (usually not as good as annuals) that generally live for two growing seasons and then die. They spend their first year maturing, and may not produce any flowers. During the second season, they will bloom for extended periods. Often they will self-seed, so you may not have to buy replacements.

They are effective when massed or tightly grouped since the flowers are their primary aesthetic attribute.

Perennials

These plants endure year after year, laying dormant during the winter months and reappearing in the spring. They usually have a limited (1-4 week) flowering period, but are widely used because they don't require frequent replacement and their blooms can be quite spectacular. Since perennials rarely maintain blooms throughout the growing season, you should focus on their shape, texture, and foliage color as well as their blooms.

Massing and grouping are common arrangements.

Bulbs

Like perennials, bulbs bloom for a short time during the growing season. Unlike perennials, bulbs can survive (when dormant) for extended periods without soil or water. Bulbs are usually chosen for their blooms and generally are used to compliment an existing, longer lasting floral display. Spring bulbs (so-called 'hardy' or 'true' bulbs) bloom while your other plants are maturing, thus giving you some early garden cheer.

Bulbs are either massed, tightly grouped, or naturalized by scattering them and planting them where they fall.

Succulents

These include Cacti and other plants that store water in their leaves or stems. They generally prefer desert or tropical sites, although some adapt well to cooler climates. They require little water and generally like full sun conditions. Specimen planting, grouping, and massing are all good choices for planting succulents, depending on their size and shape.

Plant Names

Most of the time we refer to plants by their common names, and if we could we would use them all the time. They are easy to remember, easy to pronounce, and they are familiar to us. Still, there are times when common names aren't good enough: some plants have no common name, and there are times when common names change from region to region. There are even cases where a common name for a plant in one region is the same as a common name for a *different* plant in another region. Lastly, you may need to look up information on a plant, only to find the reference book has plants listed by their so-called Latin names. That's when you'll need to use proper botanical plant names.

Common vs Latin

We aren't going to provide a list of botanical plant names. What we will do is briefly explain the botanical naming system to give you a working knowledge of it.

The botanical plant naming system, developed by Carl Linnaeus in the 18th Century, is called a binomial classification system, a big phrase that means that the plants have two-word names. The first word picks out the plant's *genus*, the generic group of plants that your plant belongs to, and it is always a capitalized noun. The second word identifies the plant *species*. A species is a subset of a genus which includes all plants of a particular kind (for instance, all broad-leafed plants), and the species name will be an uncapitalized adjective.

Genus and Species

Example: *Juniperus horizontalis* (Creeping Juniper) The genus (*Juniperus*) identifies the plant as a juniper, and the species (*horizontalis*) describes the plant according to its horizontal spreading habit.

You may find a few variations on the basic plant name:

- A botanical plant name with two species names separated by an 'x' indicates a hybrid.

  Example: *Abelia* x *grandiflora* (Glossy Abelia)

- The initials 'var' after the name indicate a natural variant of the plant.

  Example: *Salvia azurea* var. *grandiflora* (Blue Sage)

- Single quotation marks around a plant name or the initials 'cv' indicate a cultivated variety.

  Example: *Dicentra spectabilis 'alba'* (White Bleeding Heart)

- The terms 'variety' and 'cultivated variety' are often used interchangeably. They are a subset of a species which has been singled out for a particularly desirable quality. Often the cultivar has enhanced hardiness or a longer bloom time.

Plant Selection

A few tips for dealing with nursery staff

Remember: the more information you have about your site, the better the chances of getting meaningful help. Armed with the skills and data you gathered from working through this handbook, you can ask better questions, have a better idea of what you're looking for, and give the salesperson enough information to better answer your questions. Instead of saying "I have a shady area in my yard. What can I do?", you can (for example) say "I have an area that is part shade (it receives 3 hours of direct sunlight per day), the soil is slightly acidic (a pH of about 5.5), is a heavy clay loam that gets compacted very easily, and there is a lot of wind with little structure to protect it. What plants would you recommend?"

Find knowledgeable employees. Nurseries often hire part-time help, students, and otherwise inexperienced people who are just learning the nuances of gardening. Most of what they can tell you is basic information, so try to find the expert on the staff—most nurseries have at least one.

What to look for when selecting plants

In general, your best bet is to buy only healthy-looking, shapely plants. Plants that are droopy, wilted, discolored, or lanky will take longer to mature and require a lot of nursing. Look at the whole plant, sometimes wounds are hidden beneath the foliage. Healthy plants will transplant better and mature faster.

When choosing plants in containers avoid those with lots of roots growing outside of the container as they indicate a crowded root system that may inhibit healthy growth. This is especially pertinent for woody plants that may develop a

deformed root system, which contributes to a fast rate of decline.

When choosing balled and burlapped
plants look for crowded roots, for the
reasons stated above. Plants with ex-
cessively hard root balls may have
trouble extending their roots into the
soil. In all cases, handle balled and burlapped plants carefully.

With bare root plants there isn't much to
look for other than a healthy-looking root
system—the more roots, the quicker the
plant will adapt to its new garden.

When buying woody plants (mainly trees)
look for any evidence of wounds. If the bark has been gashed,
scraped, or cracked the tree may have a shortened life span.
Wounds to a woody plant don't heal; rather, they get covered
up by the outer bark. Once covered up, rot can form inside
which contributes to deformity or early death (the technical
name for this process is 'decline'). Also, if you see abnormal
looking bark at the base or anywhere on the trunk it will usually signal a wound.

When buying non-woody plants look for a generally healthy
appearance, and beware the presence of weeds in the pot.
Large weeds growing close to the roots can be difficult to
pull without harming the plant. Also, plants that are not in
bloom will usually transplant better than those with blooms.

Note:

Contrary to what people usually think, buying larger plants does not insure that your garden will mature faster. Research shows that over extended periods plants that are smaller when purchased exceed the larger ones in growth. This is especially relevant when buying trees.

Putting it all together

In this chapter we gave a very basic overview of plant types, plant names, and how to choose healthy plants at the nursery. Your goal should be to:

❑ Choose appropriate plants for your **site** and **style**. The more you know about plants the more creative you can be, so learn as much as you can about plants.

❑ Be sure the plants you select are healthy with few (if any) visible signs of damage or stress. The healthier your new plants are, the fewer problems you will have when starting your garden.

Part II

The Process

- *Design*
- *Preparation*
- *Previewing*
- *Planting*
- *Maintenance*

Design

Up to now we have discussed principles and techniques for evaluating your site, designing gardens, and selecting plants. In this section we take up the process of actually creating your garden. The following steps should get you started:

(1) Determine the conditions in your garden site by doing site analysis. Compile a list of your site constraints.

(2) Sit down and think about your wants and other constraints.

Think about your wants:

Do you want to enhance a view or terrain feature? Do you want a colorful garden or maybe a garden that is relatively free of maintenance? Do you want an in-ground watering system? What existing features do you want to incorporate into the design? Which existing features do you want to get rid of? (The list goes on.)

Think about your constraints:

What are your site conditions (your biggest and most important set of constraints)? What can you afford? How much time and effort can you afford to invest? Do you need to get e.g. a lawnmower to the site? (you'll need access, storage) Can you reach the site with a garden hose? (plants need water) Can you maintain the site? (complex gardens need a lot of maintenance) Is there some future project that has to be incorporated into the design? (like a pool, deck, gazebo, etc.) These are just a few possible constraints.

(3) Look at the existing conditions and determine what stays and what goes. You may just want to add a few perennials, or even totally change the site from the ground up. If you decide to remove a lot of existing features—especially trees—consider the effect such a removal will have on your site conditions.

(4) Make a sketch of your design, and develop your theme. Think of how you want to arrange things, and which plants you want to use.

(5) Once you have a rough sketch you'll need to calculate the number of plants you need. Find out the spacing requirements of the plants, and then either **(a)** draw your sketch to scale (1"=10'), include the proper spacing of the plants, and estimate based on your drawing; or **(b)** measure the actual planting locations in your site based on the plant spacing requirements and mature size calculations. Put stakes where each plant should go, and count the stakes.

If you are an experienced gardener you can walk through the garden site and estimate the number of plants you'll need by visualizing them in mature form.

(6) Finalize your plan and make sure you've satisfied all of your wants and constraints. Double check placements, and make any last-minute changes in your design.

(7) Prepare the site (**next section**) and buy your plants.

Preparation

Unless you are already endowed with good soil and a ready site, you will need to prepare your soil for planting. Preparation involves laying out your site, removing anything that has to go, making beds, and amending and grading your soil. Depending on your design and your site, this could be very easy work or long, involved work. Whatever the case, thorough preparation on your part will pay big rewards later. Below are some important details and hints to help you prepare your site.

Bed Preparation

First, a word of caution: As we mentioned in Part I, before you prepare your garden, be sure to check the depth of your soil. You don't want to discover that there is bedrock 3 inches below the surface *after* you have stripped the grass from your future perennial bed!

Outline the bed using stakes, a hose, or powdered lime.

If the proposed bed is currently part of your lawn: cut out the bed with an edger or spade, being careful to cut a smooth line along your outline. Use a spade or sod cutter to remove the grass. Be sure to remove the grass roots below the surface but try not to remove too much soil. Shake the dirt from the grass into the bed, and dispose of the grass.

Angle the spade slightly and work it under the grass.

If you have another area in need of grass, you may want to consider transplanting the dislocated grass to the new area. If you do, don't shake the dirt out of the roots (a sod cutter is best for this).

Note:

A spade will be fine for a small bed. If you have to strip a large bed, you may want to rent a sod cutter.

Your next step is to turn the soil in the bed, using either a tiller, shovel, spade, or spading fork. Try to work at least 8 inches of the soil, breaking up large clumps and removing any roots or rocks.

If the soil below the surface is compacted, you may want to try double digging to loosen it up. This is harder work, as you must turn the soil to about 20 inches deep. Still, in some cases you may find it very worthwhile.

Dig a trench down to the compacted hardpan (usually about six to twelve inches below the surface). It should be about two feet wide. Pile the excavated soil along the edge of the trench. Spread a layer of amendments along the bottom of the trench and turn the soil (*do not mix this layer with the already excavated soil*). Fill the trench with the topsoil you removed and repeat the process in the next row.

Now is the time to amend the soil. Evenly spread any fertilizers or amendments over the bed and turn the soil one more time. Then grade the bed with an iron rake, leveling and smoothing the soil.

If the bed is next to a building, smooth it out with a gentle slope away from the building to channel water away from the foundation. Take your time and try to get a good smooth grade—it will make a big difference in the quality of your installation.

If you are installing edging, in-ground sprinklers, drip irrigation, filter fabric, etc. you should do so now. You may have to re-grade after doing this.

Hint:

When using an iron rake for grading, the rake should be held close to your body and at a steep angle (between 5 and 40 degrees). By holding it at such a steep angle you will have more control over it, which in turn allows you to get a more even grade. Try it—it may seem awkward at first, but you'll soon see the results!

Woody Plant Preparation

If possible, dig a generous hole for the plant—about two times the width of the root ball or container but just as deep as the ball or container. Do not amend the planting soil or hole: research shows that doing so encourages the plant roots to stay in the hole rather than branch out. The plant becomes, in essence, a large potted plant (see **Planting**). After planting, you can spread an inch or two of compost over the top of the entire planting area to amend the soil. If you will be planting a bunch of trees or shrubs in a large bed you can prepare the entire bed as discussed earlier.

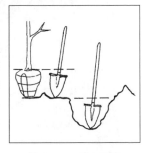

Use your shovel to determine proper depth.

Tip:

When planting in your lawn, put the excavated soil on a tarp or piece of cardboard. This will make filling and cleaning up much easier and neater.

Previewing

Place your plants (still in their containers) in the bed and space them as the label indicates using the enclosed tape measure. When measuring the distance between plants, measure from the center of one plant to the center of the next plant. Step back and take a good look at your arrangement; if you want to change your design, you should do so now. Take advantage of this preview to be sure the bed is laid out as you want it.

Be very careful to space the plants properly. They must have room to thrive, and while the bed may not seem full now you have to plan for mature plants. We cannot stress this point enough: *if you want a successful, well-designed garden, you must heed the spacing requirements of your plants.* Your bed should (in most cases) look a bit sparse when you first plant it.

One more thing: as you preview, start thinking about your planting order. You'll want to start at the back of a bed, for instance, so that you can work your way out without trampling other plants. Also, plant your big trees and shrubs first so you won't have to worry about the small plants as you are lugging the heavy ones around.

Planting

You should be ready to plant now. Follow the directions on the plant label, if provided. Use a shovel or hand trowel to dig holes. Clean-up, mulch, and water when done. The following are general instructions for different types of plants:

Balled and burlapped plants

You should remove the burlap and wire basket (if the plant has one); however, you want to remove it in the hole because otherwise the ball may fall apart before it is placed in the hole. The preferred method is to cut out the bottom of the basket and burlap so it comes out easily after the plant is in. (diagram) If the plant is extremely loose in the hole you should try to re-

Pre-cut the burlap and basket at the base of the root ball.

move the wire basket but leave most of the burlap, because trying to get the burlap off may do more harm than good. In this case just roll back the burlap on top of the ball and cut away the excess.

Cross section of a proper B+B planting.

Handle the root ball carefully—never let it drop into the hole. Gently roll it into place. Sit the plant up straight with the best side of the plant facing the viewer. Then fill around the plant and just cover the roots with soil. Gently pat the soil by hand (never stomp **on** the root ball to pack it down) and smooth the area around the plant.

Hint:

When planting near a tree you should never chop large roots. An occasional root or two is OK but never main roots (if you have to get an ax or saw to chop a root then it's a main root!). Always yield in favor of the tree, because it's probably big enough to fall on you when it dies. And it can hurt.

Tip:

When planting next to your house leave some space between the plant and the house and plan on pruning a small space between the plant and your house—this will allow air to circulate and help keep moisture from causing rot and mildew to form on your house.

Container plants

Take the plants out of their containers. In most cases they should slip out of the container easily; if not, cut the container off with a good knife or hand pruners. Knead the roots to loosen them up and place each plant in its hole. Be sure the plant sits up straight, and plant it just deep enough to cover the roots. Fill around the hole with soil, pat the soil gently with your hand, and smooth the area around the plant.

Cross section of a proper container plant planting.

Bare root plants

Dig a hole large enough to accom-
modate the plant roots. Gently
spread the roots out in the hole and
sprinkle dirt over them until they
are covered. Fill the hole up to the
base of the plant and gently pack
the soil with your hand.

*Cross section of a proper
bare root planting.*

Bulbs

Planting depths and times vary depending on the bulb, so
ask the nursery staff for planting instructions or follow
instructions on the package, if available.

Seeds

Read the package—the directions are usually clear and
planting methods and depths vary depending on what you
are planting.

Maintenance

A clean garden is not like a clean room.

A mulch will fade, weeds will crop up, and your sharp edges will blur. Your goal is not to fight a battle with nature but to work with it. Your maintenance and devotion can help your garden evolve into a complex, beautiful growth, but it should not be a chore of drudgery. You needn't polish every leaf.

Much of your gardening satisfaction will come from the way your garden evolves over time. Garden evolution is much more than plant growth; it is a process that transforms a collection of plants into a unified, harmonic garden. If you are too strict about garden maintenance, your garden won't get a chance to evolve!

Watering

New plantings should be kept moist for the first three weeks after planting unless otherwise directed. This means that you should water long enough and often enough so that the soil is consistently moist (but *not* muddy) to a depth of about six to eight inches. When planting in hot weather you may have to water more often to help establish the plants. If you notice wilting plants, water them immediately.

You can use a sprinkler or water by hand. Make sure that you water long enough for the water to penetrate to the appropriate depth. The trick is to water at a rate your soil can keep up with. If water puddles or runs off you should reduce your rate of watering or stop watering until the soil absorbs the excess water and start again. Watering in hour or half hour increments is a good practice to start until you know how fast and how deeply water is absorbed.

Be careful not to overwater. Too much ground moisture can suffocate your plants, so overwatering can be just as harmful as not watering enough.

The best time to water plants is early in the morning. The day's heat will dry the water on the plants, keeping mildew from forming. Also, early morning watering reduces evaporation. Watering in the late afternoon or early evening is the next best time. You should avoid watering during the hottest part of the day, unless you live in a very mild climate.

Note:

A good alternative to hose-end sprinklers and expensive sprinkler systems is drip irrigation. Drip irrigation reduces surface evaporation by watering plants at the ground level. This conserves water and promotes deeper root growth.

You can purchase drip irrigation systems that regulate and distribute water evenly. Many nurseries and home centers carry do-it-yourself drip irrigation kits that are relatively easy to install and maintain. The kits can get expensive, but they can also be worth the investment.

There are two styles to choose from: one has customizable water emitters for each plant, and the other has emitters spaced at regular intervals.

> **Tip:**
>
> Many people like to use inexpensive soaker hoses because they can be buried just below the surface and used as a crude drip irrigation system. Bear in mind that they are only effective to about 50 feet in length, after which they have trouble distributing water evenly along the entire length.

Mulching

Mulches are good for controlling weeds and reducing surface erosion. They also keep the ground temperature fairly constant and help the soil retain moisture, both of which make your plants happy.

There are many different mulches on the market, most of them natural and a few of them synthetic. The natural ones include various types of tree bark, shredded organic matter, and composted organic matter. The synthetic mulches are usually some sort of plastic sheeting or filter fabric.

In most cases, you won't go wrong with an organic mulch. Not only will it do what all mulches do, but it will also help enrich your soil from year to year.

When you buy a mulch choose:

How it looks: this depends on your preferences

How much it costs: It can cost a lot to mulch large areas

How much you need: If you need a lot you should buy in bulk (many mulches are sold by the yard). If you need a little you should buy it in bags.

How much work it has to do: Heavier mulches tend not to blow around in the wind and are more effective at suppressing weeds than lighter ones. Lighter mulches are good for decorative cover and for mulching around delicate plants.

Note:

Filter fabrics (also called landscape fabrics) are tightly-woven polypropylene materials that let air and moisture through while preventing all but the most persistent weeds and grasses from taking root. It is a good weed barrier but it also prevents fine silt and clay particles from plugging up drainage systems. (see Appendix 2: **Drainage Solutions**)

If you buy mulch in bulk, estimate the amount you need by figuring the area: one yard of bark mulch covers about 100 square feet (a 10' x 10' square), spread about three inches thick. (see Appendix 5: **Materials Estimation**)

Tip:

If you need a lot of mulch, check with your municipality and see if they have a community compost program for yard waste. If so, they may provide free mulch and compost; all you have to do is pick it up.

Be careful not to build up mulch around the base of plants; spread it a bit thinner around the plant base.

Smooth it, and you're done.

Fertilizing

When you should fertilize depends on many factors, especially what type of fertilizer you use, what plants you are fertilizing, and the time of year. In general, you can't go wrong using a balanced fertilizer in the spring. The following are a few basic recommendations for some plant types.

- Annual flowers and vegetables are heavy feeders. For best results, use a balanced fertilizer in the spring-time, and then use fertilizers higher in phosphorous and potassium later in the growing season.

- Perennials and deciduous flowering shrubs benefit from a higher phosphorous and potassium fertilizer after they bloom. Before then, a balanced fertilizer is fine.

- A single late fall or early spring application of nitrogen-rich fertilizer is good for most young trees.

- Bulbs enjoy a straight phosphorous fertilizing after the blooms are finished.

There are several different types of fertilizer on the market, and they come in solid or liquid form. Liquids will work faster but must be applied more often; they are most useful for plants that need a quick boost or plants that are losing a battle for nutrients with neighboring plants. Dry (granular) fertilizers, on the other hand, last longer but take effect slower. You can also choose between inorganic and organic fertilizers (see discussion of this in Part I, **Nutrients**).

The following tips may be helpful:

• If you use commercial fertilizers, follow the application instructions very carefully. For best results with dry granular fertilizers, use a broadcast or rotary spreader. there are many commercially-available broadcast spreaders, both hand-held and push-type.

• Fertilize individual plants by hand, if convenient. Apply the fertilizer in a ring approximately 5" from the base of the plant, carefully working the nutrients into the soil surface.

• Avoid getting fertilizer directly on plants (except grass!) unless the manufacturer specifically states that you can. Dry fertilizer can burn some plants if it comes in direct contact with the foliage.

• It is best to use dry fertilizers just before it rains. Failing that, watering after application activates the fertilizer and washes it off your plant's foliage.

• After applying dry organic fertilizers try to work them into the soil rather than leave them on the surface. This helps improve their effectiveness since they can be more readily processed by soil organisms.

Weeding

Weeds can turn a wonderful garden into a mess very quickly. They do not come to your garden magically; weed seeds can remain active in soil for many years. If you practice diligent weeding from the start you can make your soil relatively weed-free in a few years. Eventually, weeding will be an easy task. However, if you let them grow (even for one season!) the weeds will deposit thousands of seeds, and you'll be doing constant battle with new weeds for many years to come.

Whatever you do, don't get discouraged—weeds can be controlled with a little diligence, and weeding *is* a part of gardening. Time spent weeding is time spent out of doors enjoying your plants, and that is quality time.

Here are four ways to control weeds. Some combination of these should work for you:

Suppress:
Suppression involves prevention. Use mulches (natural and artificial) to prevent weed seeds from germinating. Mulches help keep the soil at an even temperature and moisture content which helps prevent some weed seeds from germinating.

Starve:
Many weeds thrive in adverse soil conditions. By keeping your soil well fertilized and amended you can reduce the amount of weeds that will sprout in your soil.

Stifle:
Selecting plants that have dense foliage and growth habits reduces the amount of sun underneath the plants. This in turn

83

stifles weed growth. Although some weeds will be aggressive enough to push through the foliage canopy, most weeds will remain underdeveloped due to the lack of direct sunlight.

Slay:

Quite simply, get out there and pull up any weeds you see. The sooner and more often you pull them the better off your garden will be. Some weeds will be more difficult to slay than others. For instance, many perennial weeds spread with underground root systems and you have to remove the roots to prevent regrowth. As a rule, weeds that break off at the surface will sprout again.

Deadheading

Deadheading, or removing dead flowers from plants, prevents flowers from going to seed, which in turn causes them to bloom more profusely the following season. In some cases this will even cause the plant to bloom again in the same season. When dead-

Deadheading heading, pinch or cut the dead flower at the bud or the nearest joint.

Cutting back involves cutting the flower stems on perennials for neatness.

Cutting back

Staking

Trees that remain sturdy and upright when first planted do not need to be staked. Otherwise, stake trees just enough to keep them upright and stable in harsh weather. Generally, you should not leave trees staked for periods longer than eight months; any longer than that and the tree may get damaged by the staking materials.

Perennial staking, with a bamboo stake and twist ties.

You can also stake perennials to maintain a neat appearance in the bed. They sometimes flop around, and staking holds them upright.

The common method uses garden stakes and loose twist-ties to secure plants to the stake. There are also various wire hoops you can purchase from your local nursery. If you use wire hoops, put them in place when the plants are small. Then the plant will grow through the hoop nicely.

Dividing

Dividing is done for several reasons: Often, older perennials grow poorly and dividing reinvigorates them. Dividing also keeps perennials from overgrowing or encroaching on neighboring plants. You can divide plants to increase your plant stock; you may want more of that plant elsewhere in your garden. Finally, dividing allows you to share your plants with a gardening friend!

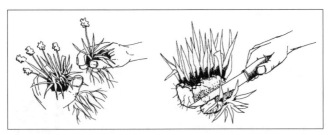

Dividing

To divide a perennial dig it up as if you are transplanting it (see **Transplanting**). Shake off excess dirt to expose the roots and separate the plant and roots into sections using either a serrated knife or your hands. If the perennial has a large tuberous root (called a crown) you can use a knife to slice off divisions of the root.

Replant the sections you want to keep, treating them as if they were new plants.

- Dividing is best done in the Spring or early Fall.
- If the plant is in bloom, wait until after it has finished blooming to divide it.

Transplanting

Here are a few guidelines for transplanting established plants on your property.

- It is generally best to transplant in early Spring or early Fall.
- Some plants have special transplanting requirements. Find out by asking a knowledgeable person at your area garden center or reading about the plant.
- Dig the hole where the transplant will go *before* you start to dig up the plant.

> **Note:**
>
> Anti-desiccants or anti-transpirants are wax-like films that inhibit moisture loss through plant foliage. They protect plants during transplanting, when the plant may otherwise lose more moisture through its foliage than it takes in with its roots.
>
> They are also used to protect evergreen plants from winter burn, which occurs when cold dry air robs plants of moisture that they can't replenish from the frozen ground. (see **Winterizing**)

- Before you transplant make sure the soil is moist so that it can help hold the root ball together.

- Use of an anti-desiccant or anti-transpirant reduces the likelihood of wilting and transplant shock.

- Adequate watering is essential: keep the soil around the transplant consistently moist for 3 weeks (longer in hot weather), then water as needed afterward.

- Do not prune branches to compensate for root loss. Minor corrective pruning is ok (see **Pruning**).

- Avoid using fertilizers for the few months after transplanting. You can use a small amount of a straight phosphorous fertilizer (bone meal, super phosphate, rock phosphate) mixed in with the backfill. If available, use a root stimulant.

Woody Plants

When transplanting small trees and shrubs, you must estimate the size of the root ball. If you aren't familiar with your particular plant's root system, this method will at least help you calculate the *approximate* root ball size: Using your

87

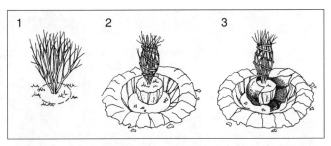

1) Determine the root ball size; 2) Dig a trench around the outer edge of the root ball; 3) Wrap the exposed root ball in burlap to hold it together.

measuring tape, measure the diameter of the plant trunk a few inches from the ground. Then measure the root ball according to the trunk diameter:

- If the diameter is an inch or less, measure 12 inches out from the trunk.

- Add an additional 6 inches out from the trunk for every additional inch of trunk diameter.

- For multi-stemmed shrubs measure 16 inches beyond the outermost stem.

It is best to have at least one person help you when transplanting larger plants, because root balls are heavy and a bit unwieldy.

Non-Woody Plants

Transplanting non-woody plants is an easy task. Carefully slice an outline around the plant, about 6 inches beyond the outermost leaves. Pry the plant out of the ground gently. If you encounter much resistance when taking the plant from the ground, slice any remaining roots underneath the main root cluster.

Pruning

Pruning can correct growth problems, remove dead or diseased wood, and maintain the appearance of your plants. As your plants mature you should prune them on a regular basis to keep them healthy and attractive. We discuss a few types of pruning below, but before we get too specific here are two general cautions about pruning:

(1) Plants often respond to pruning by sending out new growth. Whether this new growth is desirable or unhealthy depends on the cuts you make, so it is very important to make good cuts. As a rule, make cuts to branch forks or at least to a bud. Always leave a very small (quarter inch) stub to help the plant heal properly.

Making a cut to a branch fork.

(2) Good pruning is a skill, and you can only get it by practice, patience, and learning. Take your time, and step back often to look at the plant from a distance. Don't cut off too much at one time, and learn about the plants you are pruning. Since not all plants react the same to pruning, the more you know about your plants the less likely it is that you'll make a costly mistake.

Pruning back to a bud.

Thinning

Thinning allows light and air into the plant, corrects growth defects, and lets you shape plants without radical surgery. When thinning, look for and remove branches that touch or grow into each other. Remove broken, dead, or diseased branches. Remove any inward growing limbs, as well as any watersprouts or suckers. (see **diagram**)

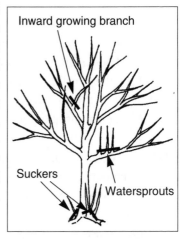

Where branches are too thick for your pruning shears, you will need a saw. When sawing, don't just lop off the problem branch—make three cuts in the branch as illustrated in the diagram. This ensures a clean cut that will heal better, and it also keeps the branch from ripping bark off the tree or shrub when it falls. The final cut should not be flush with the tree trunk; cut back just to the 'branch collar' which is the swollen ring that

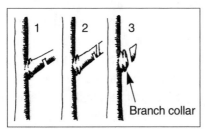

surrounds the base of the branch. If you make your cuts this way the tree can cover the wound and retard decline. It isn't necessary to coat the wound with tree paint.

Caution:

Unless you are a skilled arborist, you should consult with a tree service before removing large trees or tree limbs.

Renovating

Renovating involves drastically cutting back a shrub either to reinvigorate it or start over. In most cases renovating is needed because the shrub was not maintained properly to begin with.

Not all shrubs will respond to renovating in the same way. Some shrubs will not regrow, others take years to get back to size, and some regrow in a very short time. You should find out about the shrub so you can predict how much cutting it can survive.

- Many deciduous shrubs tolerate total renovation (being cut to the ground) and will regrow quickly. However, unless you are sure that the shrub you want to renovate is tolerant it is best to prune the shrub no more than one-third of the total plant size annually.

- Most needled evergreen shrubs cannot be renovated because they will not regrow on old bare wood.

Shearing

Shearing should be avoided in most cases because it isn't good for plants and isn't very appealing aesthetically (unless you enjoy a very simple shape, like a cube).

You can shear plants for a formal appearance, although the same caution applies here as for renovating: find out if your plant can tolerate the surgery.

Use hand shears, as they tend to be more forgiving than motorized shears. Try not to shear too much; if the plant's inner branches get exposed, you've gone too far (see **Renovating**). Gently form the plant so that it is wider at the bottom

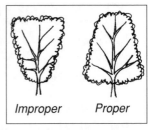

Improper   *Proper*

than at the top so the lower parts receive plenty of sunlight. This will keep the sides lush and thick.

Winterizing

In cold climates where frost and frozen ground is common throughout the winter you should consider protecting your most sensitive plants. Evergreen shrubs can be protected against winter burn by using burlap or a anti-desiccant. (see **Transplanting**)

You should wait until late Fall when temperatures are consistently cold (below 40 degrees F.) before protecting plants with burlap. With anti-desiccants you will need a day warmer than 50 degrees so it will stick to the leaves. Your best bet is to apply the anti-desiccant before the average temperature gets below 50 degrees.

For perennial gardens spread a 3 or 4 inch layer of leaves or hay over the entire bed once the ground has frozen. This will retard the repeated freezing and thawing that can kill perennials. One other type of winter protection: in areas that receive heavy snowfall you can build wooden billboard houses over woody plants that may otherwise be crushed by the weight of snow. This can be especially useful under the drip edge of a roof, where heavy snow shedding occurs. You can also tie up shrubs with twine to keep heavy snow from damaging branches.

Pest Control

A book of this scope can't begin to make you a pest control expert. We will give you some basic advice, but if you have a persistent pest problem, try to learn more about the pest and deal with it in an informed way. There are many useful sources of information you can turn to, from newspaper articles to pest control experts.

Remember this simple bit of advice: Throwing a bunch of chemicals on your plants is rarely the best way to solve a pest problem. Most of the bugs in your garden are helpful, and you don't want to kill them all. You should diminish the problem pest, but you want to avoid any solution that kills everything.

Basic pest control involves three steps:

(1) **Prevention:** Healthy plants will be more resistant to the ravages of pest and disease, so keep your plants healthy. Much of this book is devoted to helping you grow healthy plants, so if you have a problem, go back through the book: make sure your soil is healthy, your plants are appropriate for your microclimate, and they are adequately watered, mulched, fertilized. Plants under stress are much more prone to pest and disease damage, because their natural defenses are down. Prevention is by far the best way to deal with plant problems. It won't keep the most determined critters off your plants, but it will keep most problems at bay.

(2) **Identification:** Try to identify the pest. It may take some work, but often you can catch the pest at work: look under leaves, on the ground, check out the entire plant. If you can catch a pest and identify it, you have isolated your problem and made it much easier to solve. Imagine how much better information you'll get if you tell your nursery that you have Japanese Beetles, instead of saying that something is eating your bean plants!

Of course, you won't always catch your culprit. Sometimes you may think you have a bug and instead the damage was caused by a disease. Sometimes the pest only comes out when you aren't looking for it. In this case, carefully examine the evidence and make a good note of it. Often, an experienced gardener or nursery expert can recognize the cause of plant damage by looking at the effects. Even in cases where the evidence doesn't pinpoint a specific cause, you may narrow the list down to 2 or 3 likely suspects. That puts you much closer to a solution; then you can try a few different remedies that deal with each suspect.

(3) **Purging:** Once you have identified the pest you can set about getting rid of it. Start out with the simplest step: pick the insects off the plant by hand, if you can. Some pests can be controlled with home-made traps or non-toxic sprays.

Failing a simple, non-toxic remedy, try a pesticide that is specifically designed for your pest. Use it according to the directions, and that should solve your problem.

Some problems can have very effective, interesting solutions. Some may frustrate you beyond belief. Discuss your problem with several people who have dealt with it before, and read up on the pest. The knowledge won't hurt, and sometimes you'll stumble upon a remedy that is completely safe and easy to do.

A Concluding Tip

Be proud of your garden, but don't bore your friends. Gardening can be an expression of your creativity and effort. You should be proud of your work, but be aware that some gardeners turn their hobby into a game of one-up-manship. Your goal is to design a garden that is right for you, not for your neighbor. If you flex your gardening muscles too much, others won't enjoy your company or your garden. You want to share ideas with other gardeners and enjoy the learning process rather than compete with others for the best ideas.

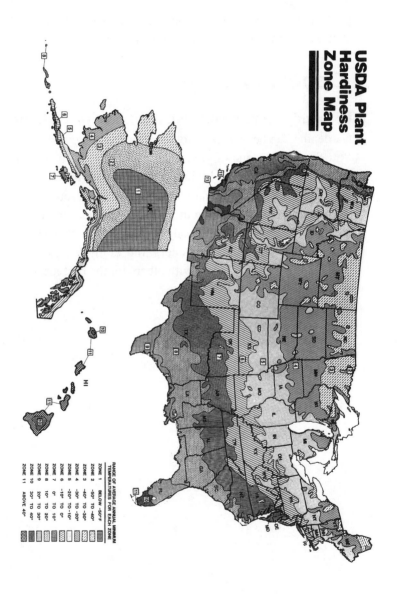

USDA Plant
Hardiness
Zone Map

RANGE OF AVERAGE ANNUAL MINIMUM TEMPERATURES FOR EACH ZONE	
ZONE 1	BELOW -50°F
ZONE 2	-50° TO -40°
ZONE 3	-40° TO -30°
ZONE 4	-30° TO -20°
ZONE 5	-20° TO -10°
ZONE 6	-10° TO 0°
ZONE 7	0° TO 10°
ZONE 8	10° TO 20°
ZONE 9	20° TO 30°
ZONE 10	30° TO 40°
ZONE 11	ABOVE 40°

Appendix 1: Special Conditions

Clay Soil

If you live in the Southeast you probably know about clay soil.

It is extremely difficult to work when wet and it is harder to work when it is dry. Try to work with it when it is moist. If you want a more workable, balanced soil, add a lot (50% by volume) of aged compost or manure. If the soil is acidic, you'll probably want to add lime as well. Eventually, the adjusting and amending will give you a soil with much better structure.

Even so, drainage and surface runoff may be a problem, because the soil horizon will be tightly packed. Consider using corrugated pipe drains (in thick clay, chimneys are not very effective) or swales to divert runoff (see **Appendix 2**). Consult with a professional if you aren't sure what to do.

Desert Soils

Arid climates have unique soil problems. For starters, they are often very alkaline. They can also have a hardpan called caliche you will have to break up. Changing soil structure by adding amendments is difficult because alkali soils rapidly dissolve organic matter. Watering often leads to the accumulation of salts in the soil (they percolate to the surface) unless there is good drainage. Raised beds or container planting is recommended, although one of the best remedies is to plant things that are well suited for these conditions.

This simple practice involves a more recent type of gardening called **xeriscaping**.

Basically it involves:

- Using plants suited to your environment.

- Using mulches to retain moisture.

- Using efficient watering techniques and devices.

- Maintaining the proper soil conditions for your plants.

Many people use native plants when gardening. Whenever practical you should use native plants; they are adapted to their regions, making them suited to the adverse conditions in your area. You may find also that they require less maintenance than other plants and attract native wildlife as well. Keep in mind that native plant species are unusually well-adapted to a specific environment in your area (such as a woodland setting or swamp). So if you decide to use them, learn about the plants and their specific growing conditions first.

Appendix 2: Drainage Solutions

Before resorting to drainage systems consider double digging if possible (see **Preparation**).

Chimneys:

These are a simple but effective way to improve drainage in areas where soggy soil is a problem, but puddles don't stand for a long time.

With an auger, post digger, or shovel dig a hole through the hard packed soil horizon. The hole needn't be more than 3 feet deep, and can be anywhere from 8 inches to 2 feet wide. Fill the hole with washed ³/₄ inch crushed stone up to the top of the hardpan. If possi-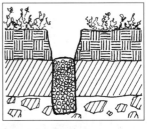

Chimney

ble, shave the top of the hardpan so that water channels into the chimney. Cover the top with filter fabric to keep fine particles from working their way into the crushed stone. Install chimneys at three to four foot intervals where needed.

Corrugated pipe drainage systems:

A common but labor-intensive method is to install corrugated pipe drainage systems, as they are good for most soggy soil and standing water conditions. They are also good for areas where excess run-off causes flooding and erosion during heavy rains because they shed water quickly.

Dig a trench about 2' deep and 1' wide. Start the trench in the lowest part of your drainage problem and continue it to the nearest area where the water can run-off to. Be sure to pick a discharge spot that will not create new drainage problems for you or someone else.

After digging the trench and making sure it has a slope of at least three inches per hundred feet of pipe, line the trench with a filter fabric, line the bottom with a 2" layer of ³/4 inch stone and then lay 4" perforated drainage pipe in the trench. Double check the slope, then cover the pipe with about 4 inches of ³/4" crushed stone. Cover the stone with filter fabric, then back fill the trench with good soil.

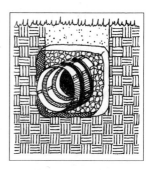

Cross section of a corrugated pipe drain.

If you have major drainage problems you should consult with a drainage expert.

Note:

Be sure you get the slope right *before* you begin covering the pipe with stone. Once the pipe is covered it will be very difficult to adjust.

Appendix 3: Plotting the Sun

One important thing you can do to help your plants thrive is determine (**a**) how many hours of sunlight your garden site gets during the day, and (**b**) how this changes over the course of the growing season. As we said in the sun section, the sun's daily path across the sky shifts higher or lower in the sky as the seasons change. To calculate this shift accurately you need to find your *latitude*, *true south*, the sun's *altitude*, and its *azimuth*.

Your **latitude** is the distance (in degrees) your garden site is from the equator. You can find the latitude nearest you by referring to the map on page 105.

True south is found by using your compass to find magnetic north (and hence south) and correcting for magnetic declination. Magnetic north is the direction your compass needle points to, and it isn't true north. True north will be a few degrees off, the exact number of degrees depending on where you are. You can use the map on page 105 to find the declination line nearest you, and that will tell you how many degrees you need to adjust to get from magnetic north to true north. True south will be 180 degrees from true north.

The sun's **altitude** refers to how high it appears in the sky from the horizon. Its **azimuth** is the number of degrees east or west of due south the sun is at certain times of the day (this is known as *solar time*). On pages 106-117 we provide pre-plotted charts of the sun's altitude and azimuth for various latitudes throughout North America. Locate the chart nearest your latitude.

Appendix 3: Plotting the Sun

Once you have the appropriate sun plot, you are ready to determine the amount of sunlight your site receives:

(1) Bring your compass, handbook, tape measure, and a pencil to your garden site.

(2) Find magnetic north using the compass, then consult the map on page 105 to find the magnetic declination line nearest you. An example: if you are in Boston you would find that true north is approximately 14 degrees west of magnetic north. Rotate the compass clockwise until the N (north) on the dial of the compass is approximately 14 degrees east of the needle (see **diagram**). Hold the compass at that point while looking where S (south) on the compass dial is pointing. Lay a stick on the ground pointing to true south, so you don't forget.

(3) Stand in your garden facing true south. Turn your head left and right, and locate any structures (trees, buildings, etc.) that will block the sun in

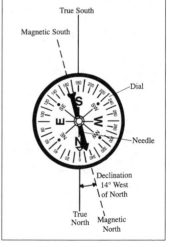

your garden site throughout the growing season. To plot the impact of each structure you will need a device to measure altitude and the compass to find the azimuth. The device can be a pencil or stick which you can calibrate in degrees.

To calibrate your pencil or stick: lay it lengthwise along your measuring tape. Mark or notch the stick at $^1/_2$" intervals along the entire length of the stick. Each $^1/_2$" segment represents approximately one degree.

(4) To find the azimuth of each structure: Face true south while holding the compass, which should also be lined up with true south. As you turn your head slowly to the left or right, stop when you come to the edge of the structure. Look at the compass to determine the number of degrees from true south you turned your head. That degree will be the object's azimuth.

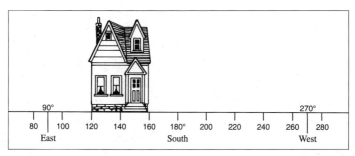

Determining the azimuth of an object in the landscape.

(5) To find the altitude of each structure: Hold the calibrated stick vertically straight out in front of you. The stick should be 2 feet away from your face (you can use the measuring tape to verify this). Align the bottom of your stick with the base of the structure, and measure the height of the structure using your calibrated notches. (For our purposes we measure altitude in degrees.)

Determining the altitude of an object in the landscape.

(6) You can then plot these dimensions on your chart and draw an outline of the structure(s). This will show you the times of the day the sun will be obstructed and when (or if) this will change over the growing season. Look at the times when the sun will be blocked. Make note of this and subtract that from the total number of hours of sunlight per day. You will then know precisely how much sunlight your site receives during the year.

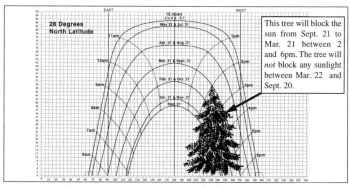

Drawing a structure to determine the time of day the sun will be obstructed and if this will change over the growing season.

Magnetic Declination Chart By Degrees

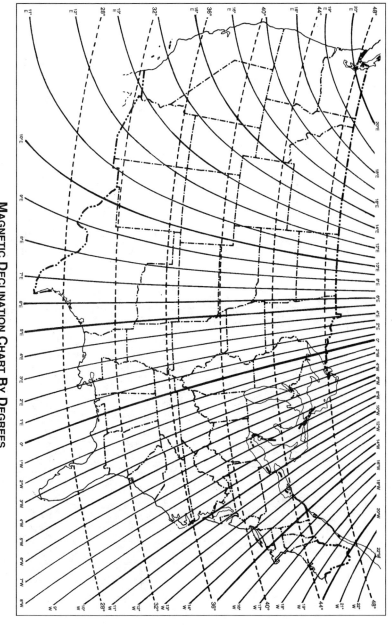

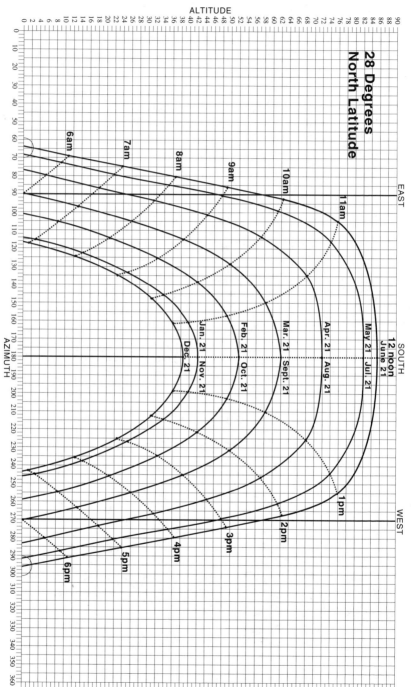

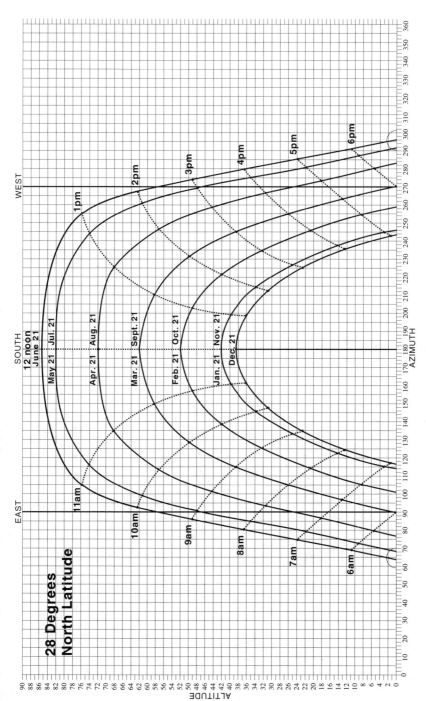

28 Degrees
North Latitude

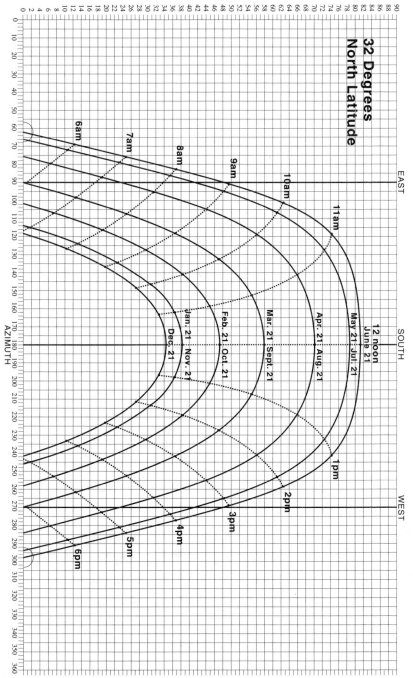

ALTITUDE

32 Degrees
North Latitude

AZIMUTH

EAST

SOUTH

WEST

6am
7am
8am
9am
10am
11am
12 noon
June 21

May 21: Jul. 21
Apr. 21: Aug. 21
Mar. 21: Sept. 21
Feb. 21: Oct. 21
Jan. 21: Nov. 21
Dec. 21

1pm
2pm
3pm
4pm
5pm
6pm

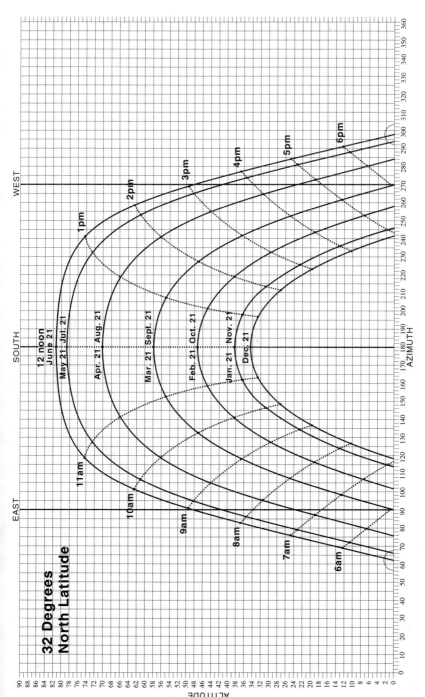

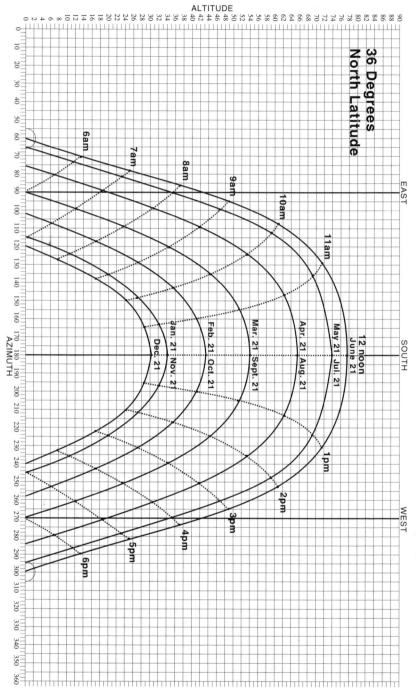

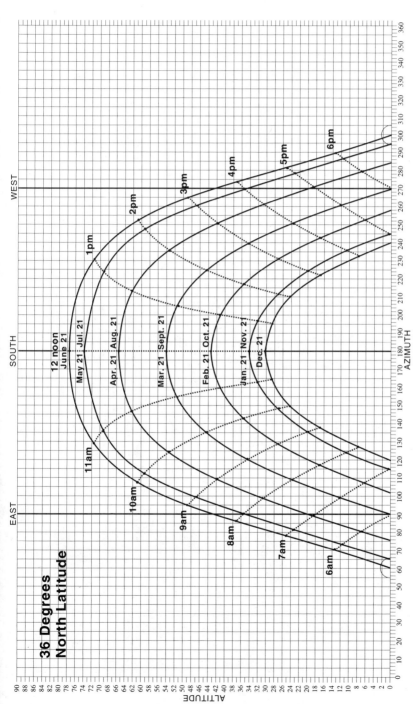

36 Degrees
North Latitude

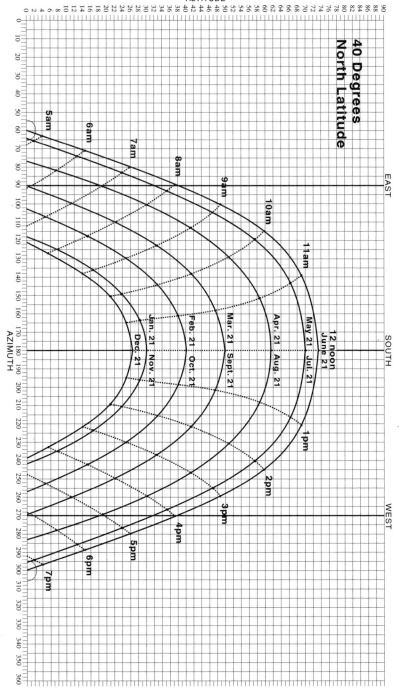

ALTITUDE

**40 Degrees
North Latitude**

EAST

SOUTH

WEST

AZIMUTH

5am
6am
7am
8am
9am
10am
11am
12 noon
June 21

1pm
2pm
3pm
4pm
5pm
6pm
7pm

May 21, Jul. 21
Apr. 21, Aug. 21
Mar. 21, Sept. 21
Feb. 21, Oct. 21
Jan. 21, Nov. 21
Dec. 21

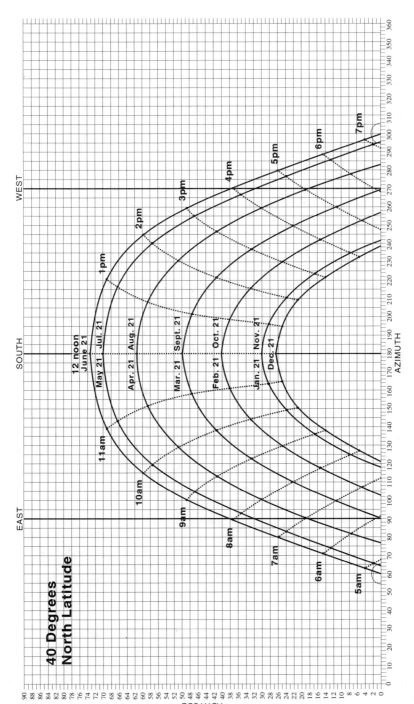

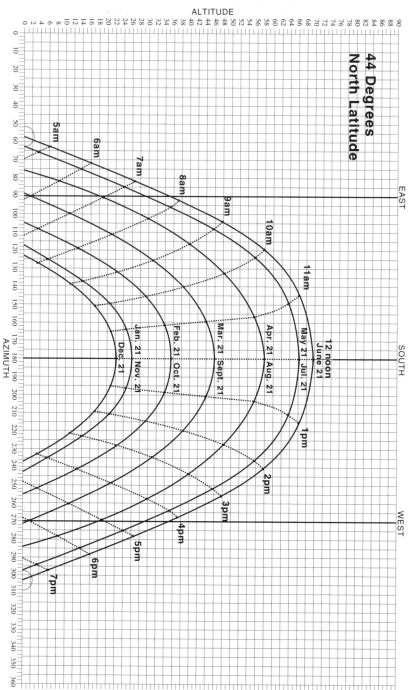

ALTITUDE

44 Degrees
North Latitude

EAST

SOUTH

WEST

AZIMUTH

5am
6am
7am
8am
9am
10am
11am
12 noon
June 21

May 21 : Jul. 21
Apr. 21 : Aug. 21
Mar. 21 : Sept. 21
Feb. 21 : Oct. 21
Jan. 21 : Nov. 21
Dec. 21

1pm
2pm
3pm
4pm
5pm
6pm
7pm

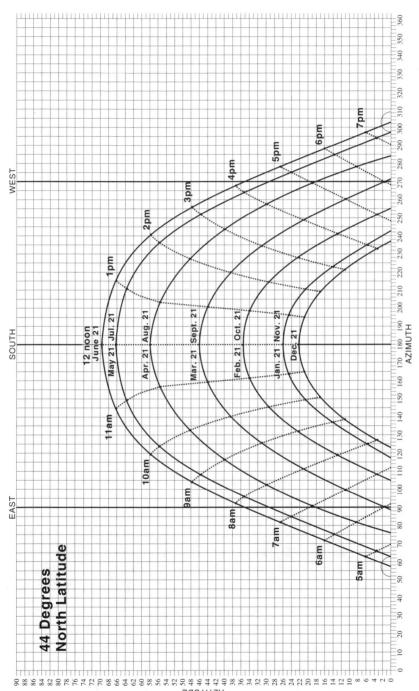

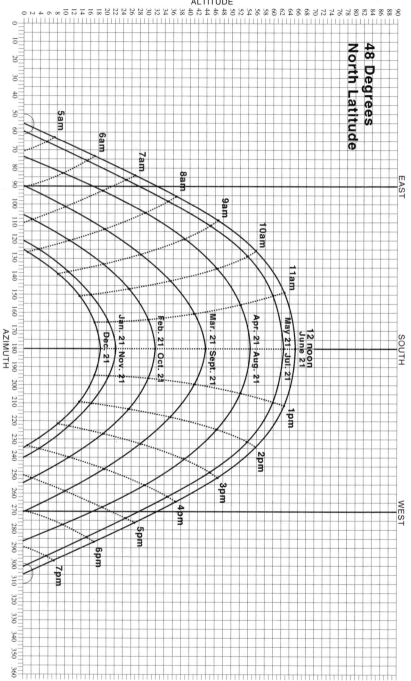

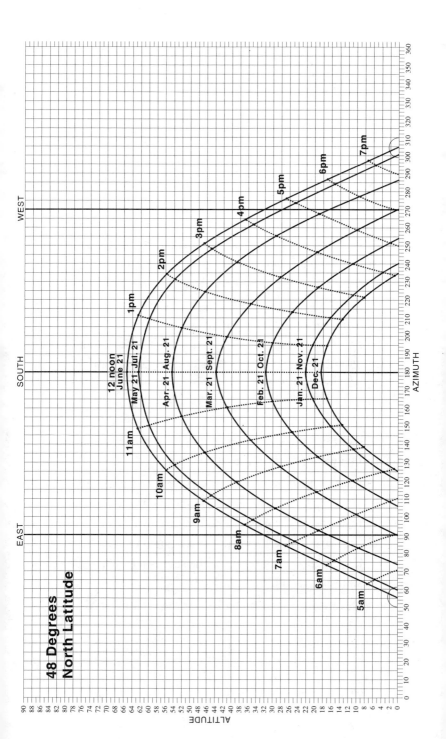

Appendix 4: Vegetable Gardens

For people growing vegetable gardens, preparation will be similar to garden bed preparation. When you create a vegetable garden consider a few things before you plant:

- Do you have full sun conditions (at least six hours of direct sunlight)? If not, you may want to grow leafy vegetables, which often fare better than other plants in shady conditions.

- Do you have enough room to plant what you want? A 10' x 10' plot will not yield a successful harvest of pumpkins, melons, and cucumbers.

- You can build up plant beds to help vegetables grow better. Mounds should be at least 5 inches high and 10 or more inches wide. Space these beds to provide walkways.

- Avoid using treated wood in vegetable gardens. The chemicals used to treat the wood can leach into the soil over time, and any chemicals in your soil are likely to end up on your dinner table.

- Use a filter fabric to cover the ground and keep weeds at bay. If you don't like the appearance, put a layer of light mulch on top of the fabric.

- Plant the tallest plants on the north end of your garden and the shorter ones on the south end so that the short plants don't get shaded by the taller ones.

- Have your soil tested by a testing laboratory, as discussed earlier.

Appendix 5: Materials Estimation

Conversions and materials estimating

Mulch, loam, compost, etc. in bulk will usually be sold by the cubic yard. Unless you need very small quantities of these things buying in bulk is your cheapest option. To determine how much material is needed you must know the square footage of the area receiving the materials and how many inches thick the layer of material should be.

Once you know how thick of a layer you need to apply, calculate the square footage of your site. If your area is a square or rectangle simply multiply the length times the width of the plot. If your site isn't square (such as a large curved bed) break it up into a series of adjoining squares until you have a good approximation of the square footage.

Multiply your square footage by the thickness of your added material measured in feet (1 inch = .083 feet). This figure will give you the cubic footage you need. To convert this to cubic yards, divide your cubic footage by 27.

For example, a 12'x12' plot needs a 3" thick application of loam.

(**1**) Multiply 12' by 12' to get 144 sq. ft.

(**2**) Convert 3" to feet by dividing by 12 = .25'

(**3**) 144 sq. ft. x .25 feet = 36 cubic feet

(**4**) 36 cubic feet divided by 27 = 1.3 cubic yards.

Soil Texture

Date	Location	Soil Texture	Comments

pH Test Results

Date	Location	pH

Amendment Application Log

Date	Type of Amendment	Location	Quantity

Fertilizer Application Log

Date	Type of Fertilizer	Location	Quantity

Notes

Notes

Notes

Notes